Date Due

DEMCO NO. 38-298

A.S.A. MONOGRAPHS

General Editor: MICHAEL BANTON

2

Political Systems and the Distribution of Power

POLITICAL SYSTEMS
AND THE DISTRIBUTION
OF POWER

FREDERICK A. PRAEGER, Publishers

distributed in the United States
by BARNES & NOBLE, Inc.

Published in the United States of America in 1965
by Frederick A. Praeger, Inc., Publishers
111 Fourth Avenue, New York 3, N.Y.
First published in 1965
© *Association of Social Anthropologists of the*
Commonwealth, 1965
Library of Congress Catalog Card Number: 65-16222
Printed in Great Britain by T. & A. Constable Ltd.
Edinburgh

*This volume derives from material presented at a Conference on
'New Approaches in Social Anthropology' sponsored by the
Association of Social Anthropologists of the Commonwealth, held
at Jesus College, Cambridge, 24-30 June 1963.*

The work should be cited as *Political Systems and the Distribution of Power*, A.S.A. Monographs 2, London: Tavistock Publications; New York: Frederick A. Praeger, *Publishers*, 1965

Contents

Contents

Contents

ix

Max Gluckman and Fred Eggan

Introduction

BACKGROUND TO THE MONOGRAPHS

The several disciplines of modern anthropology – prehistoric archaeology, physical anthropology, social or sociological anthropology, cultural anthropology, and psychological anthropology – have separated out of a general anthropology which in the second half of the nineteenth century and into the twentieth century aimed to study man both as a biological and as a social being. There are still many general anthropologists, mainly in the United States but also in Europe; and the various aspects of anthropology are still taught in many universities as a combined degree. Nevertheless, by the 1930s the different disciplines were beginning to separate from one another, though some scholars were still eminent in more than one discipline. As each anthropological discipline separated out, its practitioners turned to other subjects, whose techniques and modes of analysis were more appropriate to their problems than were those of their erstwhile colleagues. Physical anthropologists depended more on the biological sciences; psychological anthropologists (who studied the interaction of culture and personality) on psychology, especially depth psychology, and psychiatry; and social anthropologists on sociology, history, political science, law, and economics. Cultural anthropologists alone continued to draw on the biological, psychological, and sociological sciences.

Outwardly the common mark of social, cultural, and psychological anthropology was that they all continued to be comparative and cross-cultural in outlook, with an emphasis on the small-scale tribal societies of the world; and for many years the study of such a society was virtually the initiation ceremony which admitted a scholar into the ranks of anthropology. Hence all anthropologists felt they had something in common, besides their joint membership in such organizations as the

b   xi

American Anthropological Association and the Royal Anthropological Institute of Great Britain and Ireland.

We believe they had something more in common, drawn from their traditional unity, besides their previous, almost unique, concentration on the tribal societies. This was a continuing focusing of interest on *customs*, as having an interrelated dependence on one another, whether in forming cultural patterns, or in operating within systems of social relations, or in the structuring of various types of personality in different groups. This focus on customs in interdependence has continued to distinguish the disciplines of anthropology from the other subjects with which each branch is increasingly associated. The analysis of custom remains one of the distinctive contributions of all anthropological studies to the human sciences.

The extent to which anthropologists specialized in one or other aspect of the general subject varied in different countries. In Great Britain, the trend has steadily moved more and more to distinctive specialization as an archaeologist, a physical anthropologist, or a sociological-social anthropologist. In Oxford and Cambridge, where anthropology has been longest taught, regulations provide for general anthropological qualifications, but it is possible for students to qualify entirely in social anthropology and other social sciences, or at most to have minimal tuition in other types of anthropology. Compulsory training on the biological side is perhaps strongest for social anthropological specialists at University College, London. At other London colleges, and at the other British universities where social anthropology has been established since the last war, the subject has usually been placed in social science faculties or departments, with sociology, economics, and political science. In a few universities only are links strong with geography or psychology within a combined Honours degree.

The British Honours degree necessarily leads, except for the Cambridge Tripos system, to a reduction in the types of other subjects that can be taken by undergraduates specializing in social anthropology. This process does not operate in the American undergraduate schools of anthropology, and hence at that level students who wish to become social anthropologists take a much greater variety of subjects, and the anthropology they are taught tends to continue to cover several branches of the subject. This naturally influences graduate schools of anthropology, since their products have to be able to teach in more than one branch of anthropology, if they are appointed to small colleges (see Mandelbaum, Lasker, and Albert, 1963).

Nevertheless, in the United States most anthropologists are becoming as specialized as they are in British universities, and are correspondingly associating with various cognate disciplines according to their type of specialization. Owing to the greater size of the country, and the far greater number of universities and of anthropologists, there is in the United States a greater variety of types of anthropologist than in the British Commonwealth. It is in the States that cultural and psychological anthropology flourish in addition to the social anthropology, physical anthropology, linguistics, and prehistoric archaeology that are represented in Britain. The flourishing of these several branches of anthropology in the States is probably fertilized, too, by the absence of the Honours degree system: there is a more varied interdisciplinary contact, which continues beyond the undergraduate level.

The increasing specialization of British social anthropologists, with a decreasing interest on their part in prehistoric archaeology, physical anthropology, and cultural anthropology, in 1946 led the practitioners of the subject in Britain – then under a score – to form the Association of Social Anthropologists of the Commonwealth. Though they wished still to support the Royal Anthropological Institute, they considered that they had specific and limited interests, sufficiently distinct from those of general anthropology, to require the support of a specific organization. This has meant, for example, that social anthropologists in Britain have had an organized means of giving evidence on their own problems to commissions advising the British Government on higher education and research, besides evidence given by the Royal Anthropological Institute for anthropology in general. The process of *partial* separation from general anthropology continued until, in 1960, the social anthropologists joined with sociologists and social psychologists to form a new Sociology Section of the British Association for the Advancement of Science. Two of the five presidents of the Section to date have been social anthropologists. Social anthropologists still participate in the older Anthropology and Archaeology Section, but they submit more papers to, and attend in greater numbers at, meetings of the new section.

Between 1946 and 1962 the Association of Social Anthropologists of the Commonwealth increased its membership from under a score to over one hundred and fifty, even though election to membership required normally both the holding of a teaching or research post in the Commonwealth and the attainment of either a post-graduate degree (usually a doctorate) or substantial publication. Meetings of the Association in Britain ceased to be small gatherings of perhaps a dozen people, and were attended by between thirty and sixty members.

In 1962 Professor Raymond Firth, then Chairman of the Association, proposed that it should try to raise the funds to invite a dozen American social anthropologists to one of its meetings. He suggested that since the milieux in which American social anthropologists worked were so much more varied than the milieu of British social anthropologists, it would be profitable to see what was common between us and where we differed, in a series of papers on 'New Approaches in Social Anthropology'. He pointed out that though there were many individual contacts between some members of the Association and American colleagues, many British and Americans had not met one another: moreover, we had never had a joint, organized stocktaking. He further suggested that papers should be read only by scholars who had entered the subject since the war: so the phrase 'new approaches' signifies that the papers collected in these four volumes present the problems and views of a younger generation of anthropologists.

When the Association enthusiastically adopted Firth's proposal, there was no corresponding organization of social anthropologists in the U.S.A. with whom there could be discussions and arrangements. The Association therefore more or less thrust on Professor Fred Eggan of the University of Chicago the task of representing American social anthropologists. It did so for several reasons, besides his own standing as a social anthropologist. The late Professor A. R. Radcliffe-Brown, who had been for the first years of the Association's

Introduction

existence its Life President, and to whose memory this series of A.S.A. Monographs is dedicated, had taught at Chicago from 1931 to 1937. Eggan had succeeded, so to speak, to Radcliffe-Brown's position, and under the Roman rule of universal succession might be regarded as representing him. Above all, under Radcliffe-Brown's influence there had developed in Chicago perhaps the strongest single group of *social* anthropologists in the U.S.A. Eggan agreed to help organize the meeting, but insisted, of course, that his British colleagues should select the dozen American scholars whom they wished to hear. With great difficulty, the British, eventually by vote, chose a dozen from the large number they would have liked to invite. If there seems a bias to Chicago, or Chicago-trained Americans (as one or two of the others rather ironically suggested), the British are responsible, and not Eggan. The American Anthropological Association agreed to sponsor a request for support, and the National Science Foundation generously financed the Americans' journey to Britain.

The programme, to which twice as many British as Americans contributed papers, was divided into four main sections. Two to three papers were presented in a group, and discussion was then opened by either an American or a British anthropologist – again, those opening the discussions were selected from the post-war generation, though more senior anthropologists were allowed to join in the general discussion. But these Monographs are not a report on the proceedings of the Conference. They embody theoretical papers by twenty younger anthropologists, who have amended their arguments, where they felt it necessary, after listening to the comments of their colleagues. Effectively the papers present, therefore, growing-points in social anthropology as seen by a new generation of practitioners.

Two years passed between the time when Firth, as Chairman of the Association, made his original proposal, and the meeting itself, which was held in Jesus College, Cambridge, in June 1963. By that time Gluckman had succeeded Firth as Chairman, and on him, and the yet-again conscribed Eggan, has fallen the task of introducing the Monographs. It has been a difficult task: the papers cover a range of ethnographic areas and of problems which they cannot themselves compass competently.

Hence this Introduction makes no attempt to assess the substantive problems and solutions suggested in the papers. Instead, it tries to pull together the kinds of issue which crop up as interesting the contributors in several of the papers.

There was also a major technical difficulty. The papers are published in four separate volumes, covering, respectively:

1. The relevance of models for social anthropology;
2. Political systems and the distribution of power;
3. Anthropological approaches to the study of religion;
4. The social anthropology of complex societies.

Since the Introduction was planned to cut across all four volumes, we decided to write a single text and print it in each volume. Various readers may approach the series through any of the four. The arabic figures 1, 2, 3, and 4 indicate in which of the monographs is located an essay referred to in the Introduction.

SPECIALIZATION AND SPREAD:
LINKS WITH THE SOCIAL SCIENCES

The specialization of social anthropologists in a separate discipline, and the extent to which they have turned to sociology and political science, are particularly marked in these monographs. This is not surprising in the volumes on political problems (2) and on complex societies, including both peasantries and urban areas (4), where the problems dealt with are common to the three disciplines. As it happens, the other disciplines that are commonly grouped in the social sciences – economics and law – are not cited.

This is partly a matter of chance. We could provide for only a limited number of papers, and arrangements had been made to have a paper on the use of economic models in social anthropology by Mrs Lorraine Baric; but at the crucial time she went to Yugoslavia to do field-research.

Two papers do deal with 'economic problems', in the widest but not the technical sense of 'economics'. The first is by Marshall Sahlins, 'On The Sociology of Primitive Exchange', in Monograph 1. Though by its title this might be thought to deal with economic problems, its actual emphasis is on 'sociology'. It considers types of exchange in terms of degrees of reciprocity as these alter along a scale of contexts of tribal social relations, from the most personal to the least personal – if we reduce a complex analysis to a single sentence. Sahlins makes no reference to economic theorizing as such, and indeed part of the discussion of his paper turned on this point.

Eric Wolf carries out a somewhat similar analysis of morphological changes in 'Kinship, Friendship, and Patron-Client Relations in Complex Societies' (4). In this essay, Wolf examines the kinds of situation in terms of ecological and economic situations in which kinship, friendship, and patron-client relationships respectively are dominant outside the nuclear family. No more than with Sahlins, would one expect this problem to lead Wolf into the use of economic theory as such. Save for one citation from Schumpeter, he does not rely on the economists.

The absence of reference to economic theory in the papers hence means that one approach, whether it be new or old, is not covered in these four monographs. We think it is true to say that technical economics has had less influence on social anthropological research than other social sciences have had, possibly because of its highly abstract nature. In the Register of the Association of Social Anthropologists less than 3 in a 100 members list 'economics' among their special interests, and there are also few specialists in the U.S.A. Yet before the war, among other senior anthropologists, Firth, originally trained as an economist, had used the technical concepts of economics to good effect for a tribal society in his *Primitive Polynesian Economy* (1939) and, after the War, for a peasant society in his *Malay Fishermen* (1946). More recently, a number of younger anthropologists, some with training in economics, have used this training impressively. But this is perhaps more marked among those who have studied peasant societies, than among those who have studied tribes, as is shown, perhaps, in *Capital, Saving and Credit in Peasant Societies* (Firth & Yamey (eds.), 1964), a symposium containing essays by nine younger British social anthropologists, by four Americans, and by one Norwegian who was trained partly in Britain.

The Association of Social Anthropologists hopes in the near future to publish a Monograph in which the use of theoretical economics in recent work by British scholars will be considered.

When these symposia were planned, arrangements had also been made to have at least one paper on problems in the field of law. Illness prevented P. J. Bohannan from preparing this. The absence of any treatment of tribal law, and more generally of processes of social control, does not reflect the extent to which these problems have interested social anthropologists in recent decades, particularly since the publication of Llewellyn and Hoebel's *The Cheyenne Way: Conflict and Case Law in Primitive Jurisprudence* (1941). That book, and Hoebel's earlier work, inspired a number of studies on jurisprudential problems, particularly on juristic method in the judicial or arbitral process, among both American and British social anthropologists. This work has drawn largely, if sometimes indirectly, on American sociological jurisprudence. This field of research is therefore not covered in the Monographs.

Here, then, are two social sciences not drawn on for this symposium.

References outside those to the work of social anthropologists are clearly most numerous to sociologists – for example, to sociometric work and to the work of the sociologists Ginsberg, Homans, and W. F. Whyte, by Adrian Mayer in his treatment of 'The Significance of Quasi-Groups in the Study of Complex Societies' (4). J. Clyde Mitchell in the same volume discusses 'Theoretical Orientations in African Urban Studies' and he begins by stating that 'differences in behaviour as between people in the town and in the country have for long been the topic of study of sociologists and other social scientists in Europe and America . . .'. Though Mitchell cites only a few of these sociologists, their work clearly has influenced not only Mitchell, but also the numerous other anthropologists who have studied urban areas in Africa and who are cited by Mitchell.

But it would seem that, leaving aside Durkheim, whose school's influence on social anthropology has always been marked, the influence of Weber on younger social anthropologists in recent years has been considerable. If anything, that influence is under-represented in these essays: it has been very marked in a number of monographs, as in L. A. Fallers's *Bantu Bureaucracy* (no date: about 1956). With the influence of Weber – and partly inspired by his writings – goes the influence of Talcott Parsons among modern sociologists.

Perhaps the most cited and influential of modern sociologists in these monographs is R. K. Merton. His discussions of levels of theory, and of the distinction between manifest and latent functions, have always been exploited by anthropologists; and Melford Spiro uses them in his essay on religion in Monograph 3. But generally it is the increasing interest in the more meticulous analysis of social roles (referred to below) which inspires the writers to draw on Merton's treatment of role-sets – Ward Goodenough in 'Rethinking "Status" and "Role"' (1), Aidan Southall on roles in different political systems (2), and Ronald Frankenberg in an essay on the changing structure of roles in different types of British communities (4), use Merton, appreciatively and critically.

Parsons too has influenced anthropologists' thinking about this key concept. There are also indications of a growing importance here of the work of Erving Goffman – himself influenced by the work of social anthropologists – on how people operate their roles. Goodenough has drawn markedly on Goffman's books on *The Presentation of Self in Everyday Life* (1959) and *Encounters* (1961). Frankenberg argues that there is a convergence between the ideas of Goffman and those developed in British social anthropology, especially by Barnes, Gluckman, and Turner.

These references must be sufficient to show how much social anthropologists are now drawing on the cognate subject of sociology. The essays thus reflect, in research and analysis, the tendency in both countries for social anthropology and sociology to be taught either in one department or in closely linked departments.

The references above are to certain types of sociology. No essay makes use of demographic analysis – but Mitchell's and a couple of other essays refer to the importance of demographic analyses, which in general has been inadequately used by social anthropologists in their reports on communities. However, it is worth noting here that anthropologists such as Mitchell and

J. A. Barnes have, in their treatment of suitable problems, been contributing to theory in demographic studies.

In their Introduction to *African Political Systems* (1940), Fortes and Evans-Pritchard wrote that: 'We have not found that the theories of political *philosophers* [italics added] have helped us to understand the societies we have studied and we consider them of little scientific value . . .' (at p. 5). At least one reviewer asked why they did not draw on the work of political *scientists*. Since Fortes and Evans-Pritchard, with *African Political Systems*, virtually established 'political anthropology', their successors have turned increasingly to political scientists for assistance in their analyses. We have already cited Fallers's use of Weber's hypotheses in his study of Soga bureaucracy, and many other monographs on political problems have used Weberian ideas as well as works by those who are more specifically political scientists or constitutional historians. Every essay in Monograph 2 refers to works in political science. The most-cited work is Easton's study of *The Political System* (1953), and his article on 'Political Anthropology' in *Biennial Review of Anthropology* (1959). Easton, in Lloyd's words (4), 'took time from his studies of modern societies to examine the progress made by social anthropologists. [Easton] castigates the failure of the anthropologists to develop any broad theoretical orientation to politics, ascribing this to their preoccupation with general problems of social control, conflict, and integration and their reluctance to define the respective limits of political and other – social, religious, economic – systems. Easton offers a classification of African political systems which is based upon the differentiation in political roles. . . .'

We are tempted to point out that in the kinds of societies traditionally studied by social anthropologists political, economic, religious, and social systems are in fact often not differentiated, and to reply that political scientists have not themselves made so clear a definition of political systems. But, reviewing the essays under consideration, Easton's own suggestion about the classification of political systems in terms of differentiation in roles fits in with a main concern of recent anthropology – marked in Aidan Southall's essay on 'A Critique of the Typology of States and Political Systems' (2).

For the rest, the social anthropologist in his analysis of political problems seems to turn to whatever source, outside of anthropology, he feels can assist his specific analysis. Thus when F. G. Bailey considers 'Decisions by Consensus in Councils and Committees: with special reference to village and local government in India' (2), he uses work by Morris-Jones, a political scientist, on India; Wheare's now classic survey of *Government by Committee* (1955); a study of contemporary parties and politics in Japan; and F. M. Cornford's witty analysis of Cambridge University politics, *Microcosmographia Academica* (1908). Nicholas, in a comparative analysis of 'Factions' (2), equally uses a small number of political science studies. We are not suggesting that these writers use all – or even the most important – relevant sources from political science: indeed, we ourselves know of others they might have used. We indicate here only that there is a readiness to turn to political science, and Bailey's essay has more references to works by political scientists than to works by other anthropologists. Political anthropology, at least, is linking up with its cognate discipline: and this clearly is not difficult, since the concepts and analytic framework of political science are not too diverse from those of social anthropology. No new techniques have to be learned to master them.

SPECIALIZATION AND SPREAD: LINKS WITH BIOLOGY, PSYCHOLOGY, AND CULTURAL ANTHROPOLOGY

In contrast to this turn towards sociology of various kinds and to at least some fields of political science, plus the under-represented use of economics and law, we note relatively few references to cultural anthropology, psychological anthropology, psychology, and the biological sciences. In the volume on religion (3) there are references to the work of Margaret Mead, partly in the particular ethnographic context of Bali in which she worked with Gregory Bateson. This is in Clifford Geertz's essay on 'Religion as a Cultural System'. He begins by stating that the detailed studies of religion in particular societies which have characterized social anthropology are in 'a state of general

xxi

stagnation', suffering under what 'Janowitz has called the dead hand of competence'. Geertz summarizes the achievements of anthropological study of religion as: 'Yet one more meticulous case-in-point for such well-established propositions as that ancestor worship supports the jural authority of elders, that initiation rites are means for the establishment of sexual identity and adult status, that ritual groupings reflect political oppositions, or that myths provide charters for social institutions and rationalizations of social privilege may well finally convince a great many people, both inside the profession and out, that anthropologists are, like theologians, firmly dedicated to proving the indubitable.'

We do not believe that these summary statements at the opening of Geertz's essay are quite fair assessments of the acute and complicated analyses actually made by social anthropologists of ancestor cults, initiation ceremonies, political rituals, and the social context of myths, exemplified in the three essays on religion in specific societies in the same volume – by V. W. Turner on 'Colour Classification in Ndembu Ritual', by R. Bradbury on 'Fathers, Elders, and Ghosts in Edo Religion', and by E. Winter on 'Traditional Groupings and Religion among the Iraqw'. Geertz has himself written a notable analysis (1960) of a single society's religions.

Geertz is clearly being critical of his own, as well as of his colleagues', work, in order to plead for a much wider treatment of the general 'cultural dimension of religious analysis'. And he is not unique among younger anthropologists in feeling that the social anthropological analysis of religion by itself is inadequate. We take it that this mode of analysis is restricted to examining the role of religion, with emphasis on custom, rite, and belief, in social relations; and we believe that those who follow this procedure realize that they are not explaining 'the whole of religion'. They accept that they are analysing religion in only one of its dimensions, and that other dimensions have to be analysed by other types of discipline, using different techniques and perhaps examining other types of data. Clearly any set of phenomena as complicated as religion – indeed any social complex – for total understanding has to be subjected to investigation by several disciplines.

Introduction

We believe that most social anthropologists would accept this. Melford Spiro in his essay on 'Religion: Problems of Definition and Explanation' (3) states in his 'Conclusion' to his argument 'that an adequate explanation for the persistence of religion requires both psychological (in this instance, psycho-analytical) and sociological variables'. Religion, or family structure, or motivations, can be taken variously as independent or dependent variables. Spiro continues: 'But many studies of religion, however, are concerned not with the explanation of religion, but with the role of religion in the explanation of society. Here, the explanatory task is to discover the contributions which religion, taken as the independent variable, makes to societal integration, by its satisfaction of sociological wants. This is an important task, central to the main concern of anthropology, as the science of social systems. We seriously err, however, in mistaking an explanation of society for an explanation of religion which, in effect, means confusing the sociological functions of religion with the bases for its performance.' In his introductory paragraphs to his essay on Iraqw ritual (3) Winter makes the same clarification.

We have cited Spiro at length because it is in the study of religion that some social anthropologists have manifested a reluctance to accept that a specifically social anthropological analysis, giving an admittedly limited explanation, provides anything like an adequate explanation. The essays by Geertz and Spiro exhibit some of this feeling, which has appeared also in work published elsewhere, by Britons as well as Americans. Where they invoke psychology, not all of them follow Spiro in calling for some form of depth-psychology. The psychic framework employed may be an intellectualist one, in which the explanatory value for the observers is emphasized, as in the claim that the difference between tribal and universalistic rituals stems from the way people in tribal societies construct their model of the universe on the model they abstract from their own social relations (Horton, 1964).

Spiro and Winter clarify the issues involved. To understand religion, in a commonsense use of 'understand', [at least] both sociological and psychological explanations are required. The sociological – that is, the social anthropological – analysis alone is an explanation of the role of religion in social relations; and a psychological analysis alone is an explanation of the role of religion in the functioning of the personality. Nevertheless, we note that there is this dissatisfaction with the limited extent of social anthropological analysis in this field, which does not show in the treatment of political and a number of other problems.

Spiro's remains a general, abstract essay. Geertz's, interestingly enough after his castigatory opening, is largely taken up with a penetrating analysis of a specific situation in Java. With all respect, we believe that there is not 'a state of general stagnation' in the subject: the evidence of several monographs shows that social anthropological understanding of religion and ritual in specific societies continues to advance. Geertz calls for a study of symbols: we consider this is illuminatingly achieved in Turner's essay on colour symbolism among the Ndembu. Geertz 'slights' such well-established propositions as that 'ancestor worship supports the jural authority of elders': we consider that Bradbury's essay on the role of ghosts and spirits among the Edo, in a comparative background, and Winter's similar attempt to illuminate the specific variants of spirit-cult organization among the Iraqw, show by contrast how steady, deep, and wide is the penetration of the subject's understanding here.

Moreover, a discipline may advance by the working out logically of basic theoretical propositions, some of which are perhaps based on observation. This applies to theoretical economics and to some aspects of Parsons's theory of action in sociology. Social anthropology has not shown a corresponding development, save perhaps in some of Lévi-Strauss's analyses. Advance may also be achieved by the formulation of a series of propositions, based on observation. In the natural sciences, a number of these propositions have been cumulatively brought under a hierarchy of increasingly embracing laws. Social anthropology, like sociology and political science, has numerous propositions at the first level. It may lack widely embracing laws to cover many of these, but, like sociology and political science, it does have some theories of the middle range, as Merton (1958), with others, has phrased the situation. These middle-range theories are applied within a 'general orientation towards substantive materials' (ibid., pp. 87-88).

The kind of general approach to their data which social anthropologists have developed is illustrated throughout these essays: an insistence by most that there are interdependencies between both social relations and customs, and further associations between these interdependencies. Analysis of these interdependencies is often set in an evolutionary framework, even if it be a morphological rather than a temporal one, as the essays by Sahlins on primitive exchange (1), Wolf on kinship, friendship, and patron-client relations (4), and Mitchell and Frankenberg on the rural to non-rural continuum (4) well illustrate. The same framework is used by Lloyd and Southall, to some extent, in their essays on the typology of political systems (2). Yet social anthropology, judging by these essays, still lacks the kind of fundamental orientation found, for example, in Marxist sociology.

Individual propositions, stated baldly out of the context of this orientation, and of both field situation and corpus of allied propositions, may appear to be truistic – and hence banal. But the skill of anthropologists, like that of practitioners of the cognate disciplines, lies to a large extent still in their ability to apply, and weigh the application of, selected propositions to specific situations. This may be done within a single situation, with comparative checking implicit, or it may be done with occasional explicit comparison, or it may be done outright as a comparative study. On the whole, these procedures, and attempts to develop them with refinement of the basic propositions, appear to us to dominate these essays on 'new approaches' in the subject. The striving is after clarification; elimination of muddles; clearing away of concepts that, though once useful, now appear to be too gross and to block analysis; and the formulation of better theories of the middle range. These tendencies are marked in the essays by Geertz and Spiro, though these are also the only essays which press for, and aim at, much higher-level theories.

One attempt to formulate further theories of the middle range is appropriately referred to in this section on links with psychology and cultural anthropology. Wolf's analysis of the contexts in which kinship, friendship, and patron-client relations are respectively dominant in complex societies (4), is in some respects complementary to Sahlins's essay on the changing contexts of exchange in tribal societies (1): basically, it is *social* anthropological in tackling its problems, with the emphasis on making a living, handling relations with authorities, etc. But at the end of the essay, Wolf suggests that the varying texture of relations with kin, friends, and patrons or clients may have 'a point of encounter with what has sometimes been called the national character approach'. Examining works in this field, he is struck by the fact that 'they have utilized – in the main – data on the interpersonal sets discussed in [his] paper, and on the etiquettes and social idioms governing them'. Wolf cites three instances, and concludes: 'It is obvious that such descriptions and analyses do not cope with the institutional features of national structure. Yet it is equally possible that complex societies in the modern world differ less in the formal organization of their economic or legal or political systems than in the character of their supplementary interpersonal sets. Using the strategy of social anthropology, moreover, we would say that information about these sets is less meaningful when organized in terms of a construct of homogeneous national character, than when referred to the particular body of social relations and its function, partial or general, within the supplementary or parallel structure underlying the formal institutional framework. . . . The integration of the great society requires the knitting of these interstitial relations.'

We have cited Wolf at length because he appears to us explicitly to map in outline common ground between several of the essays which deal with what can be the social anthropological contribution to the study of complex societies. It is clearly accepted that a study of large-scale institutional frameworks such as the economic, or the administrative and political, falls to the lot of economists, political scientists, and sociologists. With this acceptance, goes the assumption, to quote Wolf again, of a possibility 'that complex societies of the modern world differ less in the formal organization of their economic or legal or political system than in the character of their supplementary interpersonal sets'. Anthropologists of all kinds have always been fascinated by the variety of human behaviour, even when they have sought uniformity and generality in that variety. So that aside from their interest in the small-scale, which fits with their techniques of observation, they tend to concentrate on those features of complex – as of tribal – societies where there are some distinctive sets of customs which require to be explained. We think this tendency shows in Bailey's treatment of committees and Nicholas's of factions in modern India (2).

This tendency is particularly marked in Monograph 4, specifically devoted to complex societies. In his essay on 'Theoretical Orientations in African Urban Studies' Mitchell begins by stating that 'in Africa, as elsewhere, urban studies raise the same questions'. He continues by stating that 'the focus of sociological interest in African urban studies must be on the way in which the behaviour of town-dwellers fits into, and is adjusted to, the social matrix created by the commercial, industrial, and administrative framework of a modern metropolis – having regard to the fact that most African town-dwellers have been born and brought up in the rural hinterland of the city, in which the cultural background is markedly dissimilar from that of the city'. After discussing social surveys and intensive studies, he distinguishes between 'historical' or 'processive' change to cover overall changes in the social system, and 'situational change', which covers changes in behaviour 'following participation in different social systems'. In dealing with both these types of change, Mitchell emphasizes the importance of relations of kinship and friendship – thus he faces the same problems as Wolf. He is then concerned to distinguish structural from categorical relationships, before passing to emphasize the importance of studying 'the network of personal links which individuals have built around themselves in towns'. Seeing problems very similar to those seen by Wolf, he suggests that the study of networks may show 'the way in which norms and values are diffused in a community, and how the process of "feedback" takes place.' In these studies, gossip, joking relations, historical antecedents, can all be taken into account.

In Monograph 4 Adrian Mayer treats, with technical detail, a similar set of problems, in an essay on 'The Significance of

Quasi-Groups in the Study of Complex Societies'. He too emphasizes the importance of networks and action-sets of relations, as against groups, and tries to clarify and refine those concepts. He applies them to an Indian electoral stuggle. He concludes: 'It may well be that, as social anthropologists become more interested in complex societies and as the simpler societies themselves become more complex, an increasing amount of work will be based on Ego-centred entities such as action-sets and quasi-groups, rather than on groups and sub-groups' – the latter being, presumably, what Wolf calls 'the formal organization' of complex societies.

Burton Benedict, in the same monograph, considers 'Sociological Characteristics of Small Territories' such as Mauritius. He sets his task as an assessment of the relation between the scale of society and: the number, kinds, and duration of social roles; types of values and alternatives; magico-religious practices; jural relations; political structure; and economic development. The first three are traditionally in the field of social anthropology. What is more significant is that in handling the last two sets of problems, Benedict emphasizes that the elites involved are small, and, though not explicitly, we are back with the problems of quasi-groups, networks, and action-sets.

Frankenberg's discussion (also in 4) of changes in the structure of social roles and role-sets in a range of British 'communities', from the truly rural to the housing-estate, hinges again on changes, in both groups and quasi-groups, which determine the structure of individuals' varied roles; but he illustrates too the urgent need to study custom, belief, and ceremonial as our specific contribution.

We see here, then, a common orientation, and a drive towards a common set of concepts, as social anthropologists tackle the problems of urban societies and of changing tribal and peasant communities. Some of them argue explicitly that these concepts developed to handle 'complex' situations, would also illuminate studies of tribal societies. These studies deal with problems which social anthropologists share with sociologists and political scientists, rather than with other types of anthropologists, and it may be that the *social* part of the title 'social anthropology' will begin to outweigh the *anthropology*. Yet there remain specific interests derived from the common tradition of *anthropology*.

Only in the study of religion do any of the contributors argue for the essential place of some psychological treatment. As it happens, the studies of kinship relations included occur only in the volume on 'the relevance of models': the whole fruitful field of study in psychological anthropology, represented by Lewinson, Linton, Mead, Whiting, and many others, is not referred to. This may be partly a reflection of who was asked to contribute, and what those invited decided to write on. Yet these essays show that there is a whole dimension of marital and parental relations which, it is accepted, can be studied without reference to psychological concomitants.

Strikingly, the feeling that it is justifiable for social anthropologists to work without reference to studies in psychology, is shown in Joe Loudon's essay on 'Religious Order and Mental Disorder' in a South Wales community (4). Loudon is a qualified medical, who later turned to anthropology. He has been trained in psychiatry, and has worked for the British Medical Research Council, on the position of the mentally ill in a community, and the community's reaction to such peeple. His research is into attitudes, yet he works with the same basic concepts as his colleagues: he analyses social roles in terms of class and social status, religious affiliation, length of residence in the district, etc., in relation to conscious attitudes, involving the allocation of culpability, assumption that mental disorder is illness, and so forth. So too in studying the religious order he is concerned with statements about the role of crises in personal relations, in so far as these affect reactions to mental disorder. He looks also at patterns of social mobility, and at the effect of these on individuals' social networks. His general mode of analysis 'fits' with the analyses we have just discussed: significantly, to handle social attitudes, he does not turn to work in social psychology.

GENERAL ORIENTATIONS

In this background of realignment with cognate disciplines, the essays show two main trends. The first is an insistence that certain concepts that were acceptable in preceding decades are now too gross to be useful, and have to be refined, or that they may even block further analysis. The second is the feeling that more work should be done to pull together, in a comparative framework, observations that are discrete in terms of subject-matter or of ethnographic milieu. Obviously, these are the two possibilities that offer themselves, aside from carrying out studies that repeat what has been done before – and we do not regard such studies as useless. One can either penetrate more deeply into an area of problems, or pull together what has already been done.

There are many new ideas in these essays, but no author has tried to put forward an altogether new theoretical approach – or even to recast the basic orientations of the subject. In making the statement, we do so with full allowance for Spiro's insistence (3) that to study religion, as against studying society, a psychological approach is as essential as a social anthropological one. Geertz pleads (3) for a new look – via philosophy, history, law, literature, or the 'harder' sciences – at religion, but he nevertheless considers that 'the way to do this is not abandon the established traditions of social anthropology in this field, but to widen them'. He still looks to Durkheim, Weber, Freud, and Malinowski as 'inevitable starting-points for any useful anthropological theory of religion'. The specific problems he deals with – suffering, evil, chance, the bizarre, ethics – are not in themselves new fields of problems, though his proffered solutions to the problems may be new.

The basic orientation in these essays is therefore still the acceptance that the events which comprise human behaviour exhibit regularities whose forms are mutually interdependent, over and above their interdependence in the personality-behaviour systems of each individual actor. As Radcliffe-Brown put it, there are social systems whose structures can be analysed. An interdependence of cultural institutions, each of which has an elaborate structure, would perhaps be the parallel Malinowskian formulation. Given this general orientation, it seems to us that these social anthropologists have a much looser idea of a social system, or of a complex of institutions, than Radcliffe-Brown or Malinowski had. A social system is not seen in analogy with an organic system, whose structure is maintained by some customary procedure, as it was by Radcliffe-

Brown. Nor is there acceptance of Malinowski's ideas of the function of institutions in relation to a hierarchy of needs: Spiro (3) specifically criticizes this approach.

These 'tight' models of social systems or cultures were abandoned by the inter-war generation of social anthropologists (see Redfield, 1955). But those anthropologists continued to worry about the nature of social systems and cultures, or the structure of social fields. On the evidence of these essays, the younger anthropologists no longer consider this worry justified: at least none of them has dealt with that kind of problem at length, or as basic to his analysis. Geertz (3) goes to some pains to discuss 'culture'. Spiro (3) has some discussion of what a system is. David Schneider, in an essay on 'Some Muddles in the Models: or, How the System Really Works' (1) considers the competing, and hotly argued, opposed views of two sets of anthropologists on descent and affinity: and he states that one cause of their disputation is that they need to be clearer about whether the theory is advanced to cover the structure of a social system, or whether it is about how the individual finds his way in that system. He feels that the argument will get nowhere, unless this point is clarified. That is, he asks for clarity on problem set, and he is not concerned with the epistemology of the subject. We hope that our younger colleagues feel that earlier disputation on the nature of social systems and social fields, or on the nature of culture, clarified the issues, if only through the substantive work done; and that the disputation was not always meaningless.

When we say there seems to be no new general orientation shown, but a determination to get on with the job with established orientations, we must mention the 'new' evolutionary school of Leslie White, represented here by Sahlins's essay on primitive exchange in Monograph 1. The evolutionary argument is not marked in this particular essay, and on the whole Sahlins's analysis is similar in structure to the arguments of Wolf about kinship, friendship, and patron-client relations (4), of Frankenberg about the association of role types with forms of British community (4), of Benedict about the characteristics of small-scale territories (4), and of Lloyd and Southall about the typology of African political systems (2). The type of argument is shown in the cautious hypothesis about primitive money which, among others, is advanced, by Sahlins: 'it [primitive money] occurs in conjunction with unusual incidence of balanced reciprocity in peripheral social sectors. Presumably it facilitates the heavy balanced traffic'. This is precisely the sort of hypothesis about an association between social variables which is commonly sought by anthropologists, and is well illustrated in the four other essays just cited. But Sahlins continues: 'The conditions that encourage primitive money are most likely to occur in the range of primitive societies called tribal and are unlikely to be served by band or chiefdom development. . . . Not all tribes provide circumstances for monetary development and certainly not all enjoy primitive money, as that term is here understood. For the potentiality of peripheral exchange is maximized only by some tribes. Others remain relatively inner-directed.'

We consider that, despite the turning against the simple evolutionary theories of the nineteenth century, some kind of evolutionary, or morphological, framework has been implicit in most comparative work in social anthropology. We say, 'or morphological', because many scholars have avoided an outright evolutionary statement in order to evade temporal implications. Radcliffe-Brown did this, but he believed strongly in social evolution. The result is that, aside from their important theses on the relation between use of energy and social forms, the new evolutionists, as Sahlins's essay shows, are trying to handle associations of concomitant variations, rather than items of culture, in somewhat similar ways to their colleagues. Nevertheless, we note that this new evolutionary theorizing is here represented only in the interstices, rather than in the central part, of Sahlins's essay.

REFINEMENT OF CONCEPTS

We have said that one main line of approach in these monographs, represented in several essays, is the refinement of standard concepts, in hopes of penetrating more deeply into the structure of social life. This tendency is marked in the several discussions of social roles. Even before Linton in 1936 advanced his definitions of 'status' and 'role', the handling of these phenomena was important in social anthropology: one has only to think of Radcliffe-Brown's concern with social personality and persona. But Linton's formulation, with the increasing interest of social anthropologists in sociological studies, focused attention more sharply on social structures as systems of roles (see, for example, Nadel, 1957). The work on social roles of Merton and Parsons, and later Goffman, as already cited, became influential. Some of the essays accept that, for certain purposes, 'role' can be used in analysis, as a general concept: but it is also subjected to a closer reexamination than almost anything else in the monographs.

This tone is set by the very first essay, Goodenough's 'Rethinking "Status" and "Role": Towards a General Model of the Cultural Organization of Social Relationships' (1). Goodenough is dissatisfied with the impasse into which we have run through the use of status and role as, to use our own shorthand, 'global' concepts, covering types of facts which need to be clearly differentiated. At the same time, he is dissatisfied with the present tendency to look at structural relationships apart from their cultural content. Drawing analogies from structural linguistics, he therefore attempts to construct a means of establishing both vocabularies and a syntax of the rules of 'roles'. To do this, he aims at a clearer specification of terms to describe the attributes of individuals and the relationships between them. He suggests, therefore, that status should not be, as he says Linton treated it, a means of reference to categories or kinds of persons, but that it should be confined to combinations of right and duty only. Social 'positions' in a categorical sense he calls 'social identities'. Each person has several social identities, and in specific situations one is selected as appropriate: this Goodenough terms 'the selector's *social persona* in the interaction'.

We are not, in this Introduction, summarizing any of the essays, and the preceding sketch is intended only to indicate the drive for the refinement of concepts which in the past have been illuminatingly employed, in order to secure more penetrating analysis. Having specified his terms, Goodenough proceeds to outline different types of situation in which these clarify relations between various egos and alters. On the cultural content side, he distinguishes the ranges of rights and duties, as against privileges and immunities – following here the terminology of the jurist, Hohfeld, which Hoebel has tried to get anthropologists to adopt. Goodenough thereupon proposes a technique by use of scalograms, to work out whether there are right-duty/ privilege-immunity clusters in particular identity relationships as seen *by single informants*. Varied cultural demands – such as 'sleeping in the same house', 'joking sexually in public' – are taken, and the informant is asked whether each demand applies in a particular identity relationship. These combine to give specific composite pictures of duty-scales. Goodenough argues that owing to limitations on the cognitive power of individuals – here is another example of an author citing psychological research – the demands, each forming a 'status dimension', must be limited in number to seven or less. He suggests that these duty-scales can be powerful instruments of social analysis, since (as he demonstrates by examples) they will allow objective measurement of anger, insult, flattery, and the gravity of offences. The last point is illustrated by a situation where breach of norm on the part of one identity justifies severe breach of duty by another. This will lead to precision in the study of single societies, and in the comparison of different societies.

This summary does not set out all the intricacies of the argument; but we have discussed this essay in order to illustrate what we mean when we say several authors see one line of advance in an increasing refinement of established concepts, and specification of others, to replace single concepts which, in their traditional global form, have outlived their usefulness. Goodenough's essay is the most explicit treatment of 'status' and 'role' in this way; but it seems to us that similar procedures are at least implicit in those parts of Lloyd's and Southall's essays on political systems (2) which aim to relate changes in role patterns with changes in macroscopic political structures. The explicit reformulation of the ideas involved in social roles emerges again in Frankenberg's essay (4) on changes in roles with 'movement' from British rural areas, through villages and small towns, into cities. Like Goodenough, he concerns himself with patterns of interaction – and he turns to cybernetics for ideas to handle these patterns. Both of them find in Goffman's searching study of *The Presentation of the Self in Everyday Life* (1959) and *Encounters* (1961) stimulus in handling the nuances involved in the complexity of daily social interaction, as against the more formal earlier analysis of roles in structural frameworks.

The same drive towards the breaking up of established concepts in order to examine more meticulously both the framework of social relations and the interaction between individuals shows in other fields. It is present in Sahlins's essay on types of primitive exchange (1) and Wolf's treatment of relations of kinship, friendship, and patronage *vis-à-vis* clientship (4), which have been considered by us in other contexts. It occurs as explicitly as in Goodenough's essay on status and role, in Mayer's article on 'The Significance of Quasi-Groups in the Study of Complex Societies' (4). Goodenough discusses the history of the concepts 'status' and 'role', and the ambiguities in their use, with difficulties that have arisen in applying them. Mayer looks equally closely at the way in which J. A. Barnes (1954) and E. Bott (1957) used the idea of 'the social network' – an idea which Barnes advanced in its present general form, and whose importance was stressed by Redfield (1955, p. 28) in a Huxley Memorial Lecture delivered shortly afterwards.

Mayer is concerned to clarify the different kinds of networks and action-sets that have to be distinguished, and also procedures for measuring their form and ramifications. As stated above, the same theme is present in essays by Mitchell, Benedict, and Loudon in Monograph 4 on the study of complex societies, and in Bailey's essay on committees and Nicholas's on factions in Monograph 2. These scholars are finding that theories based on concepts of groups, groupings and associations, and dyadic relationships, are inadequate for their problems: the network, and other forms of quasi-groups, which are ego-centred, are becoming more significant in bridging the gap between structural framework and individual action. There is clearly a close fit here with attempts to improve on the concepts of status and role. We note here too Mitchell's (4) distinction between structural and categorical relationships (i.e. between relationships set in associations and institutions, and relationships based on common attributes, such as race, tribe, and class).

The urge to clarify and refine appears also in a different context in Barbara Ward's essay 'Varieties of the Conscious Model' (1), where she considers the situation of a group of boat-dwelling fishermen in Hong Kong. These people consider themselves to be Chinese; and, Ward asks, by what model can their Chinese identity be assessed? Her starting-point is Lévi-Strauss's distinction 'between culturally produced models and observer's models. The former, constructs of the people under study themselves, he calls conscious models; the latter, unconscious models'. Ward argues that to understand her field situation, she had to take into account several conscious models – that of Chinese society held by Chinese literati, that of the group under study held by themselves, those of this group held by other groups of Chinese – as well as the unconscious, the anthropologist's, model. She examines the relationship between these models, as set in the context of different areas of Chinese society, to assess where 'the uniformity and continuity of the traditional Chinese social system' lay; and she finds it in family structures.

The demand for rethinking, clarification, and refinement runs through all the essays in Monograph 1, that on 'models'. We have cited it from the essays by Goodenough, Sahlins, and Ward. It appears as strikingly in the other essays: by Ioan Lewis on 'Problems in the Comparative Study of Unilineal Descent' and David Schneider on 'Some Muddles in the Models'. Lewis argues that if correlations are to be established in comparative work, it is necessary to measure the intensity of such a principle as unilineal descent. He attempts to do this by applying various criteria to four patrilineal societies. He comes to the conclusion after his survey that by these principles involved in unilineal descent, various societies scale differently, and hence he suggests that this kind of classification is difficult and probably unfruitful. He argues that the functional significance of descent varies too much, hence canons of descent may not be fruitful criteria. 'The lumping together of societies on the basis of patriliny or matriliny alone can only lead to confusion. The functional implications of descent are much more significant than whether descent is traced in the patri – or matri-line' – an argument advanced by Leach in *Rethinking Anthropology* (1961).

Since Lewis does not suggest alternative criteria, we take his essay to be an example of that important class of work which aims to prove that a particular line of research is fruitless. The implications of the final sentence are clear: more refined, multiple variables must be sought.

Schneider's essay is much more difficult to delineate. It deals with a heated controversy between anthropologists about relationships of descent, and relationships of marriage or alliance. The argument is complex, and difficult to follow without detailed knowledge of the background literature which is discussed – and at least one of us, a political anthropologist, frankly confesses his difficulties here. Nevertheless, for present purposes it is clear that Schneider is trying to clarify the terminological and other muddles that he considers obstruct agreement: he points out to the contestants where they are talking in fact about different things, when they appear to be talking about the same thing. For, he says, there are two categories of anthropologists involved, and though there may be differences between the members of each category, they are distinctive from the others. There are the descent theory anthropologists (Fortes, Gluckman, Goody), who look for actual groups of people who intermarry with one another, and alliance theory anthropologists (Lévi-Strauss, Leach, Needham), who are primarily interested in 'that construct or model which is fabricated by the anthropologist and which is presumed to have, as its concrete expression, the norms for social relations and the rules governing the constitution of social groups and their interrelations'. Schneider argues that aside from weaknesses in each theory, they both contain contradictions and obscurities in their formulations. Most of the disputants are not clear in their arguments with one another on how far they are erecting conceptual models, which do not refer to real segments of the society, and how far they are referring to actual segments, based mainly on ownership of property and other jural rights. He suggests that this is because each of the theories is elaborated for a different type of society. The alliance theory is formulated for systems (which Schneider calls segmental) in which marriages of women proceed always from one segment to another; the descent theory for systems (which Schneider calls segmentary) in which men in one segment can marry into a number of other segments.

Schneider feels that each protagonist is driven by the polemical situation to defend 'his type', and that leads to the 'propagation of whole-system, over-simple typologies'. His own plea is for the use of typologies for specific problems, 'not for sorting of concrete societies into unchangeable, inherent, inalienable categories'. Selection of various elements, rigorously defined, and examination of combinations, permutations, and recombinations of these elements in many constellations, will prove more profitable.

SPECIFICATION OF CONTEXT

Schneider's essay contains also a plea for the clearer specification of more limited and varying contexts of relations, in order to assess the association of variables. Similar demands are present in a number of other essays on various subjects. They appear in every essay of the Monograph 2 on political problems. Bailey, in examining the alleged value, or rather 'the mystique', of 'consensus' in committees, distinguishes what he calls elite and arena councils, the size of councils, forms of external relationships. Nicholas places factional disputes in various types of situation. Lloyd looks at a limited political problem, by classifying three polities in terms of modes of recruitment of the elite and analysing their association with four other important variables. Southall argues for 'partial analysis of partial systems', and takes as his criterion for classifying political systems the differentiation of political roles. In Monograph 3, Bradbury looks at the contexts in which Edo cults of the dead, as against ancestral cults, may be significant; while Winter, in analysing Iraqw religion stresses, much as Schneider does, that there are with reference to this problem at least two types of society in Africa.

THE SEARCH FOR THE BROAD HYPOTHESIS OR THEORY

It seems, then, that most of the contributors to this volume favour clarification, the breaking down, and the refinement, of standard concepts, together with closer specification of narrower social contexts, as likely to be a more fruitful line of advance than the search for sweeping generalizations. This is explicitly stated in a few essays, and is implicit in others. Since contributors were asked to write papers indicating where they thought new approaches would be fruitful, we believe we may assume that the essays in this series reflect the feeling of our younger colleagues, and that they did not merely submit to us essays on a problem on which they happened to be working. There was, of course, in the discussion on the papers, argument on this point: as there was plenty of abstract argument about scientific method. But it must be significant that perhaps only two out of a score of papers can be seen as arguing for a much wider treatment of a specific problem – and we are not sure that this is a correct interpretation of Geertz's paper (3) when taken in its entirety, or of Spiro's essay at clarifying the various dimensions involved in the study or religion. Both of them emphasize the close and meticulous analyses of facts in restricted contexts: their plea is rather for an increase in the disciplines whose techniques and concepts should be employed in analysis by social anthropologists.

All the essays in fact show that social anthropologists are ready to turn where they feel they can get help to solve a specific problem. But the one difference we find between British and American contributors is that the British on the whole confine themselves to a narrower range of other disciplines – those commonly grouped as the social sciences. As stated above, Loudon's essay on 'Religious Order and Mental Disorder' (4) illustrates this restriction. Turner, in his analysis of Ndembu colour classification (3), is aware of how closely his problems raise issues treated by the psycho-analysts, but he eschews involvement in psycho-analytic interpretations. The American anthropologists are readier to move outside the restricted range of the social sciences to draw on disciplines which employ quite different techniques and concepts.

CONCLUSION

Overall, then, these essays, whether they consider a single society or make surveys over several societies, show the continuing balancing of detailed, meticulous analysis of limited social fields with comparative checking that has long characterized the subject. The meticulous analysis of a single situation dominates in Turner's essay on colour classification, as it does in Bradbury's on Edo and Winter's on Iraqw religion. It forms too a core to Geertz's paper (all in Monograph 3). The comparative survey dominates Sahlins's analysis of exchange (1) and Wolf's of kinship, friendship, and patronage. Both types of analysis are strongly present in all the essays.

We have not attempted in this Introduction to discuss the argument of each essay or to assess its merits. The field covered by the essays shows that, even setting aside ethnographic specialization, a social anthropologist now will find it difficult to be competent on political problems, economic problems, domestic life, religious action, etc. – particularly as more and more is drawn from cognate disciplines. Therefore we are not competent to assess more than a few of the essays, and to do that would have been invidious. Instead, we have tried to delineate what we see as common in these new approaches, spread over a variety of problems and printed in four Monographs. Our own essay may be at least a guide to where readers can find the new leads that are being pursued by a younger generation of social anthropologists.

ACKNOWLEDGEMENTS

Finally, we have to thank, for our colleagues and ourselves, a number of people on whom this symposium has depended. Professor Raymond Firth conceived the plan and pushed through the preliminary arrangements, with Professor Fred Eggan. The Executive Board of the American Anthropological Association was kind enough to sponsor a request to the National Science Foundation which provided the financial support to enable the Americans to travel to Britain. Dr Michael Banton, as Honorary Secretary of the Association, organized the conference, and has acted as editor of the Monographs. The Fellows and domestic staff of Jesus College, Cambridge, provided a setting in which we met in great comfort amidst pleasant surroundings; and this side of our foregathering

F. G. Bailey

Decisions by Consensus
in Councils and Committees

With special Reference to Village and
Local Government in India

My interest in this question comes from two sets of experience. Indian village panchayats (councils) reach their decisions by seeking unanimity, sometimes prolonging their discussions to extreme lengths in order to find it. This liking for consensus is not confined to the traditional village councils of India (nor, indeed, to India alone in Asia[1]). Some Indians, who work in councils which have constitutional provision for a majority vote, yet feel that this method is inferior to that of consensus. Politicians in state and national politics refer contemptuously to '51 per cent democracy', usually, it should be said, when they find themselves in the 49 per cent. The same spirit pervades the new statutory panchayats, established within the last ten years in many parts of India, even to the extent of deploring contested elections. For example, in the elections held in December 1960 for the 7,394 village panchayats in the State of Rajasthan '. . . the Government of Rajasthan had declared a special grant of 25np [about fivepence] per head of population to Panchayats if their Sarpanch [chairman] and at least 80 per cent of the Panches [members] were elected unopposed; 27·2 per cent of the Panchayats qualified for this grant' (Maheswari, 1962, p. 847).

Second, my interest in decision-taking procedures was aroused by experience in committees in a university and, of course, from the wider experience of reading about committees. Some committees that I attend are generally reluctant to reach decisions by counting heads, and use a device called 'the sense of the meeting'. But other committees proceed to the vote quite

A   1

regularly, without signs of distress. Commissions appointed to inquire into a particular problem are felt to have done a better job if they produce a unanimous report than if they produce one or more minority reports. But other committees, like the Standing Committees of the House of Commons, regularly proceed to a division in order to reach a decision (Wheare, 1955, p. 123). Yet other committees, without demanding complete unanimity, move in that direction for particular kinds of decision, as when they insist, for example, upon a two-thirds majority.

In short, we are asking initially why some councils or committees[2] incline towards making their decisions by the method of consensus, while others use majority voting.

At the conclusion I shall take the argument a stage further and ask whether it is sensible to encourage consensual decision-making, as the authorities in India do, and whether the results of insisting on this procedure are likely to be in accord with other expressed policies and intentions.

THE FACTOR OF SIZE

Let us be clear, at the outset, that a decision by consensus cannot be reached in a council where *active* members number more than about fifteen. A unanimous decision in a council of one hundred men is, in fact, an act of acclamation or legitimation: the actual decision has been taken elsewhere. The very complicated and subtle process by which consensus is reached is not possible where large numbers are involved, as I shall show later.

It follows that where a large council has to take a decision (as distinct from legitimizing a decision taken elsewhere), then this must be done by majority vote.

Our interest lies in the smaller councils, and in the fact that some among these incline towards consensus, while others use the system of majority voting.

THE MYSTIQUE OF CONSENSUS

Certain ideas about human nature and about man in society, derived probably from Rousseau, have reappeared in contemporary Indian politics, and are used explicitly to justify the official encouragement of decisions by the method of consensus. In this section I shall show that we do not have to decide the truth or falsity of these ideas before discussing the structural concomitants of consensus procedure.

These ideas are put forward enthusiastically in a booklet, *A Plea for Reconstruction of Indian Polity*, by Jayaprakash Narayan (1960). JP, as he is called, is a Gandhian, a most distinguished one-time leader of Indian Socialists, both in and outside the Congress, who withdrew from party politics, joined Vinoba Bhave, and now devotes himself to social work and social reform. Narayan states his argument with a profusion of metaphor, but, I think, with clarity:

'Modern western democracy is based on a negation of the social nature of man and the true nature of human society. This democracy conceives of a society as an inorganic mass of separate grains of individuals: the conception is that of an atomized society. The brick with which the present edifice of democratic polity is constructed is the individual voter and the whole process of democracy rests on the arithmetic of votes. The Individual casts his vote as an atom of society, not as a living cell in organic relationship with other living cells. It is not *living together* that is expressed and represented in the institutions and processes of democracy, but an abstracted individual' (pp. 47-48).

The argument is supported by an account of what is supposed to have been done in ancient India:

'It is interesting to recall here that in the Indian village communities there were no elections to executive offices on the present majority-minority pattern, which is a divisive and disruptive process. Instead there was selection by general consensus of opinion, or sometimes by drawing lots' (p. 51).

The argument runs like this: communities are organisms, the parts of which are naturally adjusted to work in harmony with one another. Without the disruptive influence of parliaments and political parties and majority votes, and without the cult of the individual, communities work harmoniously. Everyone participates in decision-making and decisions are reached, inevitably, by consensus. Conflict is not inevitable and a part of human nature: it is the product of wrong institutions.

If we treat this as an argument about historical fact in India, we find ourselves, to say the least of it, on not very sure ground. So far as I know there are no accounts of events in village councils in ancient India which give the same substantial detail that we get from our own experience. We have no means of knowing how consensus was reached in those days, or on how many occasions it was not reached. Indeed, if we study early European accounts of Indian villages, we find that in general village officials who did not inherit their positions were appointed to them by feudal lords. Ordinary people had nothing to say about the matter, unanimously or otherwise.

Second, there are several varieties of an *argumentum ad hominem*, which are useful not because they prove or disprove the point at issue, but because they provide a background which helps us to understand the behaviour of people in present-day India, and, indeed, in some of the other new nations. The longing for consensus (by people like JP) is 'a most understandable reaction to an awareness of how divided and heterogeneous a society modern India really is' (Morris-Jones, 1960, p. 1031). The notion of consensus also is encouraged, the same authority suggests, by recalling the unity of purpose achieved in the independence struggle. 'It is convenient for this purpose not to have too good a memory' (ibid., p. 1031), for there were more than a few notable schisms in and outside the Congress. We might add to these two factors an aversion for the materialism of the West among the more naïve of those politicians who follow the Gandhian style, and suggest that one reason (but not the main reason) for the dislike of majority voting is that this procedure is considered typically Western.

We can file away this set of ideas about the nature of man in society, and the doubtful history with which it is buttressed. It does not matter what is the natural state of man in society – or whether it is sensible or not to ask such questions. We take up these ideas only at the point where they connect consensus procedure with one set of institutions, and majority voting with other social institutions.

One element, however, remains: not the truth or falsity of

these ideas about the nature of man in society nor the value of the historical evidence which is advanced to support them, but the plain fact that there are some Indians who accept these ideas as a generalized guide to conduct and as an ultimate value which transcends material interests. It is important to understand that we cannot point to these values and use them immediately as a structural explanation of behaviour. To say that a council strives for consensus because its members value consensus is evidently a circular argument. But it may well happen that after a thorough exploration of the rights and duties which council members have outside the chamber, and of the interests which they are serving, covertly or openly, we may still be unable to account for their behaviour except by saying that they feel it right – they are under a moral imperative – to behave in this way. At that point we have reached the terminus of structural explanation.

THE 'FACE-TO-FACE' HYPOTHESIS

Why do some councils try to reach decisions by the method of consensus more resolutely than others? One explanation may lie in the social relationship which the councillors have with those whose affairs they are managing, whom I shall call their 'public'.

We consider first the proposition that there is likely to be a premium on consensus procedure in councils in communities where relationships tend to be multiplex, because in such communities disagreements cannot easily be isolated within one realm of social action and tend to cause total paralysis. You can quarrel bitterly with your neighbour if you live in certain areas of London, Manchester, or Leeds and still get on with the business of making a living, taking part in politics, worshipping your God, and maintaining amicable relationships with your kinsmen, because all these activities have nothing to do with your neighbour: but you cannot do this in Bisipara, Tikopia, or even Pentrediwaith, because some or even all of these activities are likely to involve you with the same set of people. Pentrediwaith (Frankenberg, 1957) is a most suitable example, since the book not only attempts to document the hypothesis set out above, but also gives a uniquely detailed account of committee behaviour.

People in Pentrediwaith attempt to avoid the *open* expression of conflict, which we will call dispute. They do not refuse a request, but delay fulfilling it. The minutes of committee meetings are not detailed and the names of proposers and seconders of motions which may later give rise to dispute are not recorded. Strangers are brought into activities and manœuvred into making controversial proposals, and are afterwards saddled with the blame for the discord. The reason for this and other devices is that Pentre is a face-to-face community: '... in village conditions open and continuous breach is not possible. If it did occur it would place in conflict not only friends but different members of the same family' (p. 18). I think there are difficulties in this hypothesis.

In the introduction to the book, while developing the hypothesis that strangers take the blame for village discords, Gluckman writes, 'The end result is that the village remains a village, for the values of unity pass into the new activity: it is a village activity' (p. 5). The phrase 'values of unity' resembles Narayan's ideas about consensus: it is a mystique about the collectivity. It is not the 'values of unity', anyway, which make villagers chary about being seen to introduce conflict, but the possible consequences *for themselves*. They do not seem to value village unity as such and they seldom (except sometimes in relation to outsiders) exhibit signs of consensus: quite the reverse, for they seem to be a quarrelsome lot who like throwing eggs into the fan, so long as they are not caught in the act. For example (on p. 138), a woman swiftly withdrew a proposal when opposition was voiced, and Frankenberg comments 'if a local proposer makes a suggestion he withdraws it as soon as it shows signs of raising controversy'. It is clear from the text that the woman already knew that her proposal would cause controversy: this was her whole intention. Would it make any difference if we erased 'values of unity' and said that the 'values of quarrelling' pass into the new activity? As Srinivas once aptly remarked, Indian villagers are not face-to-face communities: the typical posture is back-to-back. In India 'different members of the same family' are often chronically 'in conflict' (and in dispute too), without feeling that their situation is impossible. 'Your brother is your enemy', the Oriyas say, and the feud which has gone on for three or more generations between related families is commonplace both there and elsewhere in India. In short, at least for Indian villages, the statement that 'in village conditions open and continuous breach is not possible' is untrue.

Some of these difficulties may be resolved if we separate two kinds of activity which are at first sight connected. (*a*) There is a range of behaviour from damping down *dispute* to allowing it free expression. (*b*) There is a range of behaviour from readiness to compromise to intransigence. I shall argue that we need not take (*a*) into consideration, when we consider panchayats in India.

(*a*) and (*b*) are not the same thing. There are examples from Pentrediwaith of utter intransigence cloaked beneath overt avoidance of verbal controversy. From the other direction we can think of examples of open and prolonged dispute terminating in compromise. We can make this separation because these two kinds of behaviour fall into different categories of action, in that (*a*) is symbolic action, or ritual, while (*b*) is substantive action.

If (*a*) is symbolic action, what does it symbolize? Specifically, what does avoidance of open disputation, in the Pentrediwaith fashion, symbolize? From the tone of the introduction to Frankenberg's book, we might be tempted to say that it symbolizes the collectivity, village unity, or something of that kind. But I do not think we need go so far. The man who avoids putting a controversial motion and manœuvres an Englishman into doing so, is symbolizing his own reasonableness. He is doing nothing but proclaiming that, unlike the Englishmen, he is not an uncouth and quarrelsome fellow, but knows the etiquette of committee behaviour and the way to conduct arguments in the Pentrediwaith idiom.

Leach remarks that English women wear a ring and Kachin women a turban to symbolize the married state, and argues that he does not have to explain why different objects are used, but only has to notice that both are symbolic statements about social status (1954, p. 16). In Indian panchayats differences of opinion are normally expressed in a roundabout and oblique way: in the British House of Commons members refer to an opponent as 'honourable', even when the substance of what they are saying indicates that they consider him dishonourable. Both these are ways of indicating to the audience that the speaker knows the appropriate etiquette: nothing more. *Every* council damps down the more violent kinds of dispute. The point is that while every council has an etiquette of this kind and could not do its work without it, variations in this etiquette do not necessarily indicate variations in substantive behaviour. An avoidance of open dispute does not necessarily mean a readiness to compromise and to seek for unanimity; nor does plain speaking, even abuse, automatically and always indicate intransigence.

Therefore the problem that we carry forward to the analysis of Indian panchayats is not the degree to which open dispute is muffled (symbolic action) but the degree to which councils seek compromise and unanimity. The problem which is central in Frankenberg's book – the muffling of dispute – is not central to the investigation of consensus as against majority voting.

SANCTIONS AND TASK

In the book on Pentrediwaith there are two accounts of a committee proceeding to a vote and reaching a majority decision. In one case (p. 94) the minority promptly organized and sent to a higher authority a petition against the decision, and blocked it; in the other case (p. 138), the secretary, who was on the losing side in the division, forgot to write the minutes and the decision was never implemented. Elsewhere in the book we read of noncooperation and the defacing of posters put up to advertise a football match, and so forth. I think it is reasonable to conclude that some of the apparent anxiety to damp down dispute is not merely from fear of embarrassment at open disagreement but is also a genuine effort to find a compromise and springs from the fact that everyone knows that if the decision is not the result of an agreed compromise, then it cannot be implemented. In other words, in such situations people seek not merely to damp down dispute, but rather to resolve conflict.

Much the same is true of the traditional panchayats in, for example, Bisipara. Such panchayats have no effective sanction to quell a substantial dissident minority.

It follows from this that conflicts will tend to be resolved by compromise if the majority know that the minority must be carried with them on pain of taking no action at all. This will apply whether the council is operating in a community with multiplex relationships or whether the members never see one another outside: for example, a dramatic society, which has no sanctions other than the extreme one of expulsion, with the consequent risk of dissolution.

These arguments apply especially to those councils which, besides being legislative or judicial bodies, must also be executive bodies implementing decision. If the decision is implemented by a separate executive, it becomes much more difficult for the disgruntled minority to block it. If they themselves are part of the implementing body, then they need only withhold their cooperation. All the committees in Pentre, other than perhaps the parish council, were their own executives. So also, for the most part, are traditional panchayats in India. Broadly speaking, in such communities the greater the division, the less effective will be the decision, and 51 per cent democracy would certainly mean inertness.

I suggest, therefore, that, other things being equal, a council will seek for compromise and consensus, if the majority would have no sanctions to implement its decision.

In turn this suggests that a leaning towards compromise or towards majority voting will be influenced by the task which faces the committee. Those committees which determine policy are likely to allow opposing points of view to be put forward, and not to be primarily concerned with finding compromise. But committees with an executive function, faced with a deadline for action, are likely to have a means of resolving conflict in a mechanical fashion, typically by a majority vote.

ELITE AND ARENA COUNCILS

It sometimes happens that a committee which has just taken a decision by a majority vote will vote again on what is essentially

9

the same proposition but in slightly different words, and this time return a unanimous decision in favour of the motion. Such a proceeding is typical of an elite council.

Elite councils are those which are, or consider themselves to be (whether they admit it openly or not), a ruling oligarchy. The dominant cleavage in such a group is between the elite council (including, where appropriate, the minority from which it is recruited) and the public: that is to say, the dominant cleavage is horizontal. The opposite kind of council is the arena council. These exist in groups in which the dominant cleavages are vertical. The council is not so much a corporate body with interests against its public, but an arena in which the representatives of segments in the public come into conflict with one another.

Other things being equal, arena councils will not damp down dispute and will come reluctantly and with difficulty to compromise, if they do so at all, because each councillor (or each group of councillors) is steered by the heavy rudder of those whose interests he represents, and to whom he is answerable. But the elite councillors have no such rudder; they are likely to come into conflict, but they have a strong incentive to present a front of consensus and keep their ranks closed in the face of their public.

An example of an arena council is a Standing Committee of the House of Commons, set up to consider the details of a particular bill. A nucleus of twenty members is chosen from each party in proportion to the seats which it holds in the House. Then up to a further thirty members may be selected, the intention being to involve people who show a concern in the subject-matter of the bill. In all cases the government has a majority on the committee. Members of each party sit on opposite sides of the room. The discussion is not the 'round-the-table' affair that we associate with committees, but consists of speech and counter-speech just as in the larger body. The debate is guided by the minister or his deputy on the government side, and by his 'shadow' on the opposition side. There are acts of compromise by which the bill is modified (especially as the proceedings of such committees do not receive wide publicity), but undoubtedly the main object of the procedure is to give a

thorough airing to opposed points of view, and the usual mode
of reaching a decision is by division; that is, by a majority vote
(Wheare, 1955, p. 123). The Standing Committees are, therefore,
an example of an arena council. Their dominant mode for interaction is freely expressed conflict of opinion and the formal lines
of conflict are derived from cleavages in the larger body. There
are, of course, informal links across the floor and these may well
shape the bill, but the deciding vote reflects the cleavages in the
larger body. (I may also repeat that a truly consensual procedure in a body of between twenty and fifty people would not
be possible, for reasons which will shortly be given.)

For an example of an elite council, I take that kind of committee which consists of the heads of departments in a faculty
or in a college within some British universities. Let us call them
'the guardians'. It is a commonplace that such committees try
to take decisions by 'the sense of the meeting'. Why do they do
so?

There are several answers. First, such groups set a high value
on rationality and behave as if there is an objectively correct
solution to every problem: that is, they have as an article of
faith the belief that if they argue constructively they will eventually agree upon the correct course of action. But this is a value
explanation which belongs logically not at the beginning but at
the end of our exploration. Second, there is a variant of the face-
to-face hypothesis. It is not that guardians avoid open conflict
for fear of what their assistant lecturers will say when they get
back to the department (in any case their doings are confiden-
tial), but rather that they must be wary of trampling too heavily
on one another's corns, because they require favours of one
another in other spheres and on other committees; a mode of
social interaction which the perceptive Cornford calls 'squaring'
(1908), p. 22. It is to be noted that a consensual decision reached
through squaring is only possible when a small number of people
are concerned, and when they interact with one another in
several different situations. We are not saying that this frequency
of interaction *enforces* a consensual decision: only that the
'horse-trading' negotiations which can lead to consensus are
only *possible* when there is a frequency of interaction.

Finally, the members of an elite council have a common

11

interest, which is one basis of their endeavours to reach unanimous 'sense-of-the-meeting' decisions. If questioned, a guardian would certainly say that the common interest was the well-being of the society which they govern (that is, the faculty or the college). Arguments round the table usually have this as their explicit or implicit starting-point. The majority batter down the minority in the name of the common good, and when, in return for some concessions, the minority withdraw and allow a unanimous decision, this too is done in the name of the common good. But the common good at the end of the last sentence is not the same as the common good at the beginning. The common good which the minority preserve by their withdrawal is the good of closed ranks among the guardians. This is given occasional explicit recognition, but always in the context of an argument that rulers divided among themselves are likely to be bad rulers and thus the common good (first sense) will suffer. It is never explicitly said that this closing of the ranks is an act of fusion consequent upon the opposition between the guardians and their subjects. I am not, of course, saying that every unanimous decision is a result of this structural opposition between rulers and ruled: only that on occasions this opposition can be one factor promoting sense-of-the-meeting decisions in councils of this type. Behaviour of this kind is evident in some of the statutory panchayats in India.

Elite councils and arena councils are ideal types, and we need to ask of actual councils not which of the two types they are, but rather to what extent or on what occasions they are one rather than the other, and whether there is any sustained movement from one pole towards the other. A committee of workers may be charged with the task of negotiating working conditions with a committee of employers. When both sit together they become an arena committee. But the management committee is an elite in relation to its larger body, the shareholders, and it therefore has an internal incentive towards closed ranks. Faced with this situation, workers' representatives are also inclined to become an elite. Their external relationships (*vis-à-vis* management) promote fusion between segments and factions within the workers, but at the same time create and widen the horizontal cleavage between union leaders and members.

EXTERNAL RELATIONSHIPS

We can use this same example of labour negotiations to state a proposition which is obvious, but important. Any council, whether elite or arena, will tend towards closed ranks and at least present a façade of unanimity when acting in opposition to a body outside itself and its public. I give one example taken from *The Times* (London) of 27 February 1963:

> 'An agreement to call an electoral truce during the forthcoming local elections was announced at Tipton, Staffordshire, last night. This is to enable Tipton council to concentrate on its opposition to the absorption of the area by West Bromwich, as proposed by the boundary commission.'

SUMMARY

If we now take together considerations of both task **and** structural position (internal and external), we arrive at the following scheme:

A	B
Councils lean towards consensus when they have one of the following characteristics:	Councils proceed readily to majority voting when they are
1. an administrative function, especially when they lack sanctions *or*	1. policy-making, *or*
2. an elite position in opposition to their public, *or*	2. arena councils, *or*
3. concern with external relationships.	3. concerned with internal relationships.

It is important to read this scheme rightly. It does not mean that the only councils which strive for consensus are those which also have the three characteristics of being administrative, elite, and concerned with external relationships. The three characteristics are conceptually separate from one another: they cannot be derived from a single principle. We can conceive without contradiction of an elite council (A2) taking a policy-

13

making decision (B1) about a matter internal to the society (A3) – e.g. university guardians deciding whether to put their money into building or staff – and, other things being equal, consensus is likely to be difficult in such circumstances. Equally we can conceive of an arena council (B2) taking an administrative decision (A1) concerning external relations (A3) – e.g. a county council deciding *when* to approach the ministry for assistance in establishing a new university. In such a case they are more likely to reach consensus than when they were deciding whether or not to ask for a university, and, if they got it, in which town it should be located.

This is a formal statement and has the usual clarity that such statements can achieve. Life is more complicated. It is complicated not only because the same council may exhibit different combinations of the six characteristics on different occasions, but also because some of these six characteristics may provide a repertory for argument in the council chamber. An unwary minority may concede a policy decision if it is presented to them as merely the best way of administering an agreed policy. Conversely, it is a not uncommon device for those unable to present a rational argument for the administrative decisions they prefer to push the argument back by making it 'a matter of principle'. Nevertheless, confusions of this kind do not render the three pairs of characteristics blunt as tools of analysis.

The concomitants of unanimity which we carry forward are these:

(a) *Executive tasks.* When a council has to take action it is likely to seek an agreed solution. This is especially true when there is no separate executive machinery. It is even more the case when there are no sanctions to enforce the decision.

(b) *Elite.* When a council sees itself in opposition to its own public, it is likely to close ranks.

(c) *Pressure from outside.* When a council sees itself in opposition to an external body, it is likely to close ranks.

Now let us go back to the problem with which we started. Some of the Indian States in local government legislation are attempting to encourage decisions by consensus. In the next section I shall show, among other things, that where this campaign is pursued, it will be successful in so far as the local government councils have the characteristics (*a*), (*b*), and (*c*) above. Second, where these characteristics exist, an insistence on consensus procedure will tend to perpetuate them. Third, these characteristics are the very reverse of what the establishment of representative local government is intended to bring about.

TRADITIONAL PANCHAYATS IN INDIA

Representative local government (based on a restricted franchise) has existed in India in a fragmentary fashion for several decades. I do not here take these earlier experiments into account because local government institutions established in the fifteen years since independence are based on total adult franchise, are widespread and, intentionally at least, ubiquitous. They seem likely to affect the structure of Indian society more profoundly than their predecessors of the British period. There is little connection, genetic or morphological, between the earlier and newer forms of statutory local government.

But in many areas there is a strong link between the traditional village panchayat and its modern successor, and to understand the way in which the latter works, we have to know something of the former. Everywhere in India where traditional panchayats are reported effective power is said to be, or to have been until recently, in the hands of a dominant caste. It is also often reported that the energies of traditional panchayat members go largely into factional disputes, especially in villages where the dominant caste is numerically large in relation to other castes. These factional disputes often cause total paralysis, and such panchayats appear as arenas where there is an endless disputation about decisions which are seldom taken and, if taken, rarely implemented. Are these panchayats to be considered (1) administrative or policy-making, and (2) elite or arena councils?

I think, although I have not space to prove it, that traditional village councils during the period of British rule were only rarely engaged in administration. Village affairs were directed either by tradition (dates and organization of festivals, management of temples, cleaning of public areas, etc.) or were in the hands of the administration (law and order, collection of revenue, etc.). Other villages were in the control of a landlord. This is not to deny that there were some effective traditional panchayats (Bisipara certainly had one), but only to say that life could go on in most villages even where the panchayat was reduced to total inertness by factional disputes. It would be wrong, therefore, to think of the traditional village councils primarily as administrative bodies.

But it would also be wrong to see them as policy-making bodies. Those Indian villagers who use up their energies in faction-fights often dispute over matters which, from an objective point of view, are trivialities. Panchayats in such villages are, or were, merely arenas in which the players scored points off one another in what was literally a game of politics.

Are they, then, arena councils? Certainly opposing points of view are given an airing. Yet they are not arena councils because the members are not steered by cleavages in the public: members are not, so to speak, constantly looking over their shoulder to see what their constituents will think of them. Factions in the dominant caste may command an army of retainers and subordinate allies in inferior castes, but these people do not constitute an interest represented by men of the dominant caste. They are rather a weapon at the disposal of the faction leaders, in just the same way as skill in debate might be a weapon. In this case the dog wags the tail: in the proper arena committees the tail wags the dog.

Nor are traditional panchayats elite councils. The characteristic of being elite is defined by a relation to the public. But the traditional panchayats are not opposed to their public: indeed, the latter does not count. Traditional panchayats, therefore, are neither elite nor arena councils but simply councils without any larger body.

STATUTORY VILLAGE PANCHAYATS

After this brief survey of traditional village councils, I shall outline the intentions of the government in creating statutory panchayats.

There were three main intentions. First, the authoritarian bureaucracy, inherited from the British, was to hand over much of its power to freely elected local government bodies. The bureaucracy, so national and state politicians claimed, had proved too inflexible to adapt itself from the requirements of mere law and revenue to those of economic development and social reform. Second, it was thought that the programme of self-help which the government had designed for rural communities would be implemented with more enthusiasm if the people felt that they were governing themselves. Third, there were frequent complaints that the existing 'establishment' in the villages got the benefits of community development at the expense of the underprivileged. It was hoped that future development, channelled through freely elected local government bodies, would solve all these problems.

Legislation varies from one State to another, but one can construct a general picture without claiming that it is universal. There are three tiers of councils. At the bottom are village panchayats, usually considerably larger than the existing traditional panchayats and covering a population of roughly 5,000. The chairmen of these panchayats constitute, together with some other persons, the intermediate tier of Panchayat Samitis. At the top level there are Zila Parishads, covering usually a district, and also consisting of the chairmen of the lower-level Panchayat Samitis together with other persons.

The statutory village panchayats differ in several important ways from the traditional panchayats. First, most of them cover more than one village. Second, being linked with development, they dispose of important spoils. Money and contracts are routed through them, *via* the higher-level councils. Consequently their disputes are no longer about trivialities. Third, and partly as a consequence, they are charged with definite and sometimes very complicated administrative functions. Fourth, since these councils are intended to be chosen by free election, there is at least the possibility that they will become related to a public, and become either elite councils or arena councils.

At present most new councils have the characteristics that are associated with consensus. First, they are not designed to discuss general policy, but rather to implement policies handed down from above. In fact, many of them take a fundamental policy decision, more or less covertly, in reversing the socialistic policies decided for them. But, this apart, the councils are expected to implement, either directly or through sub-committees, settled policies, and as such they must incline towards muting conflict and, when conflict arises, seeking compromise.

Of course, there are some decisions, in the course of putting policies into practice, which must be taken by the council and which concern internal affairs, and these are likely to give rise to the expression of conflicting opinions. When only one road, or one well, or one school is to be built, they must decide where it is to be located. But a large section of panchayat work concerns outside relationships, and tends to keep the ranks of the council closed. They may be in competition with other village panchayats for scarce favours. They are also intent upon blocking the levelling tendencies of socialism; they do not want a redistribution of wealth and they fear the upsetting of the established rural elite.

Many new councils are in fact an old elite established in new forms. People elected to positions of power on the new councils are also people who held power in the traditional councils of earlier days. Sometimes they are chosen freely by a subordinate majority, because important men seem most likely to get the best bargain from outside administrators and politicians. They may also get themselves elected by preventing the election from being free. In some places election is by a show of hands: even where there is a secret ballot the poorer villagers may not believe that it is secret, and lay themselves open to economic intimidation or direct violence. Where lower castes do assert themselves, they may be worsted in various 'undemocratic' ways. In short, there is fairly widespread evidence that at least some of the councils are beginning to think of themselves, in relation to their own electorates, as elites and rapidly close their ranks when a threat to their dominance appears from below.

In these circumstances paying a bonus for an uncontested election puts yet another weapon in the hands of the existing dominant group. It is easy to make out that upstarts from below or the occasional renegade from the ranks of the dominant caste are upsetting the applecart and preventing the team from winning the prize. So far from consensus being a sign that everyone in the village is of one mind and one heart, it may be a sign that the dissidents either feared to enter the ring at all or had already been worsted by crooked means beforehand. 'Consensus is a fair name for what may be an ugly reality' (Morris-Jones, 1960, p. 1031).

In such circumstances the underprivileged are not likely to feel that they are governing themselves and not likely to become enthusiastic about working for village development, when all benefits go to the wealthy. What is needed, in fact, is not consensus but more conflict: a situation in which leaders have to look over their shoulders all the time and answer their supporters.

Obviously the story does not end there. The scheme for investigation sketched out above needs to be tested more systematically both on the traditional panchayats and on the new statutory panchayats. There are also other problems which require investigation, some to round out the present scheme and others arising from it.

In the first category I need to look more closely at the internal structuring and rules of procedure of councils, in particular at the job done by the chairman and by the secretary. Second, a close analysis of the actual steps by which disagreements give place to unanimity or are terminated by voting, either in one meeting or over a series of meetings – the tactical rhythm, so to speak, of committee behaviour – would be useful. Third, the alternatives of consensus as against majority vote need to be supplemented by consideration of other forms of decision-taking: by drawing lots, consulting oracles, and appealing to the gods in one way or another, at what we might call the 'consensus end of the scale' and, at the other end, by examining a number of complicated variations in voting procedure.

Once we have a number of reasonable suggestions which connect behaviour in councils with structural characteristics in the wider society, the way is open for a comparative historical and perhaps, if one dare say it, evolutionary study of decision-making.

This essay, as the reader will have realized, is hardly to be called 'work in progress', still less a finished study: rather it is a programme for research.

F. G. Bailey

NOTES

1. 'Decision making, Japanese style, is based upon consensus. There is still a deep feeling in many quarters that it is immoral and "undemocratic" for a majority to govern, for decisions to be reached without compromise with the minority' (Scalapino & Masumi, 1962, p. 145).

'. . . [in Java] matters are not decided by voting. The aim is rather to secure essential unanimity . . .' (Jay, 1955, p. 226).

2. What I have to say in this essay applies to both councils and committees, unless I indicate otherwise. There is a clear difference between the two in theory: the council is superordinate and has sovereignty; the committee has its task and the power it possesses delegated to it from above. But in practice the difference is not so sharp. It is not difficult to think of bodies which have the title of committee, but which in fact have no more than a nominal responsibility to a superior. For convenience I shall generally talk of councils, but this is to be understood as a general word for both committees and councils.

A second difference is that a committee meets in private, whereas a council may debate before an audience. This difference is clearly likely to affect members' behaviour towards one another, and it is considered, in various contexts, in the course of the essay.

REFERENCES

CORNFORD, F. M. 1953. *Microcosmographia Academica*. Cambridge: Heffer.

FRANKENBERG, RONALD. 1957. *Village on the Border*. London: Cohen & West.

JAY, ROBERT R. 1955. Local Government in Rural Central Java. *Far Eastern Quarterly* 15: 215-227.

LEACH, E. R. 1954. *Political Systems of Highland Burma*. London: Bell; Cambridge, Mass.: Harvard University Press.

MAHESWARI, B. 1962. Two years of Panchayati Raj in Rajasthan. *Economic Weekly* 14: 845-848.

MORRIS-JONES, W. H. 1960. The Unhappy Utopia – JP in Wonderland. *Economic Weekly* 12: 1027-1031.

NARAYAN, JAYAPRAKASH. n.d. (*circa* 1960). *A Plea for Reconstruction of Indian Polity*. Wardha.

SCALAPINO, ROBERT A. & MASUMI, JUNNOSUKE. 1962. *Parties and Politics in Contemporary Japan*. Berkeley: University of California Press.

WHEARE, K. C. 1955. *Government by Committee*. Oxford: Clarendon Press.

Ralph W. Nicholas

Factions: a Comparative Analysis

Comparative politics is a variety of research usually conducted by political scientists and aimed at comprehending structures and events of significance for the governments of entire nation states. Nowadays it is customary for students of this subject to include one or more non-Western governments in their comparisons. Local politics, another subdivision of political science, has remained largely a Western enterprise, practiced by Westerners on small-scale political arenas found in their own countries. Social anthropologists have a well-established concern with small-scale non-Western political institutions, but comparison (when it is admitted as a legitimate method) has been confined to similar and related tribal political systems, largely in Africa. By this means, the study of *institutional* politics, systems in which principles of recruitment and alignment are relatively clear, has progressed. Such studies generally place only as much emphasis upon political *process* as is consonant with an interest in political structure. My study of politics in some Indian peasant communities, however, and preliminary comparison with descriptions of politics in other peasant societies, suggest that social anthropologists may be able to make contributions to general political studies and comparative politics by elucidating small-scale, non-institutional political processes in non-Western societies. This paper deals with 'faction', one kind of political process which I found it necessary to understand in analyzing the politics of Indian peasant villages. In studying faction one must, as Professor Firth (1957, p. 294) says, leave 'the well-trodden ground of conventional structural analysis for a type of inquiry which is from the outset an examination of "dynamic phenomena".'

The faction is a troublesome form of social organization – troublesome because of the frequency with which it appears in primitive and peasant societies, and because it is so refractory

21

to the usual analytic methods. Here, by comparing several different cases of factional development and conflict, I attempt to analyze factions as a special form of political organization. I have studied factional politics in two distinct kinds of society: the reservation society of the Six Nations' Iroquois Confederacy in Canada, and some peasant villages in India.[1] Most of what is said here about the social organization of factions and about the relationship between factionalism and political change derives from these societies. In order to determine the essential principles of factional organization – to give a sociological definition of 'faction' – I have drawn on published cases of factional politics in five different societies and social institutions. A number of social scientists have commented upon various aspects of factionalism, and I shall attempt to examine some of their views in one or another of the sections into which this paper is divided: (I) definition, (II) social organization, and (III) political change. Before taking up the sociological definition of the phenomenon, however, I would like to make clear two important assumptions.

Lasswell (1931, p. 51) points out that 'the term faction has been employed as an opprobrious epithet in the political field since Roman days. . . . A faction seems to subordinate the public good to private gain, and thus the term takes its place in the dialectic of political struggle especially as a means of defense and counterattack by those in power'. It seems hardly necessary to indicate that, for present purposes, I shall use the word 'faction' in the most neutral sense possible. Some observers of factional politics, though their interests are scholarly, seem to have permitted the emotional load of the term to influence their thinking about factions. Thus, it is common to find factions connected with a 'breakdown' of social institutions, rather than treated as an expectable alignment of personnel in certain kinds of political fields, or regarded as one mode of organizing political relations under conditions of rapid social change.

There are, broadly speaking, two ways of approaching factions which lead to different though equally useful results: one approach focuses on the analysis of political conflict, the other on the analysis of political organization. Students of political organization, such as Oscar Lewis (1958, pp. 113-154), may count the number of factions present in a community, and

22

explore the reasons for the persistence over many years of discrete, identifiable factions.[2] Those who are interested primarily in conflict place emphasis upon the transitory character of factions and assert with Scarlett Epstein (1962, p. 139) that 'it is not the number of factions that is important, but rather the way hostilities between opposing factions are expressed. In any one dispute there can be only two opposing factions and a neutral one'.[3] I disagree with Lewis's contention that factions may have important social functions outside politics; as Firth (1957, p. 292) says, factions 'operate for the most part in the political field or with political effects in other fields'. At the same time, my analysis aims primarily at an understanding of political organization rather than the nature of political conflict. Factions cannot, of course, be separated from conflict, but it is not conflict in which I am now most interested.

I. A SOCIOLOGICAL DEFINITION OF FACTION

I have tried to separate the distinctive from the incidental features of factional politics by comparing reported instances of factions from five different kinds of society and social institution. A brief sketch of each of these five cases is presented, followed by a set of five propositions, derived from analysis of the cases, which I consider to characterize factions and to distinguish them from other kinds of political grouping.

(i) *A wandering Pygmy band.* The BaMbuti, described by Turnbull (1961), is a Pygmy group living in wandering hunting and collecting bands in the Ituri Forest of the Eastern Congo. The band described consisted generally of about 100 persons, three patrilineal groups with a few affines attached to each. Turnbull relates three instances of conflict in the band. In one case the leader of the smallest of the three groups was threatened with the expulsion of his group from the band (pp. 99-100). In the second instance, the leaders of the two major kin groups divided their camps for a time (pp. 237-238). The third conflict, however, did not invite simple recruitment of supporters along kin lines because the disputants were brothers. The man who was originally wronged began, one day, to name friends and relatives who would support him in punishing his brother (pp. 107-109); immediately the band's censure shifted from the offender to his belligerent brother who 'was guilty of the much more serious crime of splitting the hunting band into opposing factions'.

(ii) *A village-dwelling African tribe.* The Ndembu, described by Turner (1957) live primarily by shifting cultivation and hunting. Villages, ordinarily groups of ten or eleven huts with two or three persons resident in each, may be composed of a headman, his brothers, their wives and children, the headman's sisters (with their children) returned to the village after divorce, and a miscellany of other persons attracted to the village by the influence of the headman. Although residence among the Ndembu is virilocal, descent is matrilineal, so that a village headman's sister's son might succeed him (pp. 76, 87-88). Under such a system many conflicts over succession developed, both between senior and junior claimants, and between established and aspiring political leaders. During the course of his work Turner witnessed several crisis situations during which 'the whole [village] group might be radically cloven into two factions' (p. 91). The distinctive feature of these factional conflicts, which sets them off from conflicts in a segmentary lineage system, is that the conflict groups changed in composition owing to 'transferences of persons fron one faction to another, loss and replenishment in the followings of leading men' (p. 131). Here, clearly, is political recruitment and affiliation which could not be managed under only the principles of a kinship system.

(iii) *An overseas Indian community.* In areas such as Fiji to which large numbers of indentured Indians, drawn from the poorest rungs of Indian society, have been brought, there is virtually no indigenous authority system. Peasants were transplanted from several different cultural and linguistic regions of India and left to settle in politically 'decapitated' communities after the abolition of the indenture system in 1916.

When Mayer (1961) studied it in 1951, Vunioki was a village of 514 persons who were members of three cultural groups: Hindus descended from South Indians, largely members of a single kinship group; Muslims, most of them members of two kin groups; and Hindus descended from North Indians, comprising two principal kin groups and thirteen homesteads outside these groups (p. 36). These groups provided the raw material for recruitment to factions in Vunioki. The cleavage between Muslims and Hindus in India is customarily referred to as a 'communal' division, while that between speakers of different languages, on a broad scale, is known as 'linguistic regionalism'. Expectable conflicts of this kind are not so interesting here, since the organization of support follows a single clear principle, just as in the case of kin-group conflict in tribal societies. This does not mean that political recruitment in Vunioki does not follow the lines of cultural and kin groups, but conflict in the community is not about the differences between Hindus and Muslims, between speakers of Hindi and Tamil, or between kinship groups. The fact that political competition in the village is neither communal nor kin-based means that support may be recruited across these important lines of cleavage. Factions in Vunioki seem to radiate from an intense schism, cross-cutting kin lines, within the Southern cultural group. These factions developed originally over a land dispute between two brothers (pp. 122-125).

Mayer found a number of reasons for joining factions in Fiji Indian villages: an important factor was simply 'individual benefit, expressed in the repayment of obligations or the support given in anticipation of favours', either often strictly economic on both sides. Ties within the kin and cultural groups were multiple and strong, and could be used to bring fellow members into a faction. Balanced against the advantages of factional membership, however, were the disadvantages resulting from the hostility of opposing factions – which meant that there were some neutrals in every dispute. Of course, the merits of any case might place a man in one camp or another, 'but the recruiting power of the subject matter of a dispute, though considerable at any particular time, was less lasting than the motives of benefit' (pp. 135-136).

(iv) *An Indian peasant village.* The village of Namhalli in Mysore state had a population of 615 when Alan Beals (1959) studied it in 1952 and 1953. Namhalli had, in contrast to

Vunioki, a plethora of leaders, both traditional and government-sponsored (pp. 429-432). Yet, like Vunioki, politics in Namhalli operated on the basis of factions, two or three of which seemed always to be present in the village (p. 433). There were seventeen different castes resident in the village, each of these being made up of several kin groups, but 'the basis of the faction cannot be established by reference to previously existing traditional groupings. The faction need not represent opposed castes, a conflict between progressives and conservatives, or a conflict between economic groups'.

Factions in Namhalli were built up from several 'cliques'. The most ordinary kind of clique was composed of a family, its affines, and its servants. Small, tight-knit caste groups might also act as cliques. Groups of friends who, for example, had been schoolmates might make up a clique. 'In nearly every case, cliques included relatives, friends, and persons bound together by economic ties, such as employee-employer or borrower-lender relationships' (pp. 433-434). Members of 'politically dominant cliques' were likely to enter into any village dispute and make it a context of factional struggle. The relations between two leading factions consisted 'of boycotting each other and of trying to create incidents which would cause some or all members of the other faction to lose money or property' (p. 436).

(v) *The Japanese political parties.* The Japanese Parliament consists of a Liberal Democratic majority and a Socialist opposition. Each of the parliamentary groups, however, is actually a federation of factions, of 'multiparties constantly in flux' according to a recent study by Scalapino and Masumi (1962, p. 81). The factions are 'leader-follower groups' in which roles are well defined: followers give their support to the leader in parliament and in intra-party struggles; 'the leader has the primary responsibility to provide positions, funds and other necessities of a good life'.

A faction leader utilizes old school connections, long-standing ties of friendship made in former offices, and mutual interests, to recruit members of his faction. Questions of ideology, policy, and mutual tactics enter into factional affiliation, and they do so to a greater extent among Socialists than among Conservatives. But at the bottom, all factional ties are personal between leader and follower and are based upon an assessment of mutual self-interest (p. 101). Political competition is primarily factional competition, and 'the activity and energies of the members are largely taken up in this struggle, because it determines the individual fortunes of the members. . . . Factional loyalty becomes the primary loyalty. . . .' In a footnote to this, the authors observe that 'each faction is organized as a club'; each club has a name, and factional coalitions organize themselves similarly and take a name. The dominant coalition within either party is generally known as the Main Current group, and it is opposed by the anti-Main Current (pp. 79-80).

There are several other instances of factional politics which could have been treated here. I would like to have increased the range of social institutions represented to include, for example, factions in a bureaucracy and in a trade union. The five cases presented will, however, assist in getting a grasp of the fundamental nature of factional politics. By distinguishing the common features from the local peculiarities, it is possible to specify some of the essential characteristics of this political phenomenon. I state what I think these characteristics to be in the form of five propositions.

1. *Factions are conflict groups.* In all the cases presented the conflict of factions is at least implicitly obvious. In fact, it is during social conflict that factions emerge out of a sociologically undefined background to give the observer a view of their personnel. Certainly, factions are visible more constantly in the Japanese political parties than in the peasant villages, and more visible in the villages than in the tribal societies. Still, it is certain that factions would not exist in the Japanese parties without conflict, just as they would not in a BaMbuti band – conflict is the *raison d'être* of factional membership. Conflict explains why there is no such thing as *one* faction in any political arena; obviously, there must always be at least two factions. I shall not attempt now to deal with the process of factional development, except to note that it seems to be through some kind of dialectical process that two or more factions can come about simultaneously in a field.

2. *Factions are political groups.* This proposition simply specifies the kind of conflict in which factions engage. If we regard politics as 'organized conflict about the use of public power' (Curtis, 1962, p. xxiii), then it is factions which organize this conflict in certain kinds of society and institution.[4]

3. *Factions are not corporate groups.* This negative criterion is important since it points out a basic difference between factional and other kinds of political conflict. Anthropologists are accustomed to deal with political conflicts between enduring corporate groups such as dual divisions, clans, or lineages; political scientists study conflicts between corporate political parties. Factions seem to lack the permanence of any of these kinds of group. Even in the extreme case of the Japanese parties, where factions are institutionalized in the form of clubs, it seems clear that the next generation of parliamentarians will not provide personnel for the same series of factions their seniors now possess. In fact, on the basis of the example provided by ex-Prime Minister Nobusuke Kishi's faction, it seems that one of these groupings may not outlive its leader (*The Times*, 2 November 1962). That factions are not corporate, that they are basically impermanent, does not mean that they may not persist for a long period of time; Beals traces the Namhalli factions back to 1920. The lifetime of factions among the Ndembu was limited by secession; the most extreme result of any factional struggle was the withdrawal of one faction to form a new village, which would then presumably lack factions for the time being. The only instance of factionalism in the BaMbuti band was very ephemeral indeed, being crushed in its incipient stage. There seems to be a regular gradation of societies along a scale of complexity according to the degree to which there is institutionalization of factions.

4. *Faction members are recruited by a leader.* Although such concepts as 'membership' and 'recruitment' must be understood broadly when speaking of factions, they are matters of primary sociological importance here as in the study of institutional politics. Members can be connected to a faction only through the activity of a leader, since the unit has no corporate existence

or clear single principle of recruitment. The leader who is responsible for organizing the personnel of a faction is ordinarily a man with more political power than any of his followers. He is not usually a leader with 'charisma', the Weberian 'gift of grace' which motivates political supporters on a level above narrow self-interest. To use Nadel's (1951, p. 99) term, the 'pointer relation' which marks a man as a member of a faction is an effective social display of allegiance to the leader – speaking or fighting on the leader's behalf, joining the leader's club, voting as the leader tells him, or whatever other functional political act is regarded as appropriate. Leadership may be provided not only by a politically powerful individual, but also, as Beals suggests, by a 'clique' based in an influential family. Another kind of clique might be composed of several leaders, each of whom has a modest following, but none of whom is individually capable of mobilizing an effective unit.

5. *Faction members are recruited on diverse principles.* A faction leader ordinarily has several different kinds of connections with his followers; he makes use of all possible ties to draw supporters into his faction. This proposition is closely related to Firth's (1957, p. 292) observation that the bases of recruitment to factions

'. . . are usually structurally diverse – they may rest upon kin ties, patron-client relations, religious or politico-economic ties or any combination of these; they are mobilized and made effective through an authority structure of leader and hench-man, whose roles are broadly defined and whose rewards in many cases depend upon the leader's discretion.'

The importance of various kinds of connection binding members to the leader will become clearer in the next section.

II. THE SOCIAL ORGANIZATION OF FACTIONS

I turn abruptly now from comparison of the most general kind to detailed examination of factional politics in a single Indian peasant village. This case study is intended to clarify by concrete example the meaning of the five abstract criteria which I hold to be sociologically significant in defining factions and in distinguishing them from other kinds of political conflict group. Particular emphasis is placed here upon the continuity of conflict which keeps factions alive and maintains their personnel in surprisingly unchanging alignments over long periods of time. The social characteristics and roles of faction leaders, and the means by which supporters are recruited, are examined in some detail. To explain the dominant political cleavages leading to the pattern of factions I saw in this village in 1960 and 1961, I begin the story of social conflict about 1910 and bring it up to the time of the 1960 village council election. This election constituted a kind of political crisis, like the crises found by Turner (1957, p. 91) among the Ndembu, during which 'the pattern of current factional struggle' is revealed. At the time of the election the political alignment of almost every villager became apparent because each leader utilized every possible connection with other villagers to bring support to the candidates of his camp. Before sketching in the history of conflict in the village it will be useful to outline very briefly some of the principal characteristics of the village.

Govindapur village
Govindapur village is located in the deltaic eastern portion of Midnapore District, West Bengal. It lies about sixty miles southwest of Calcutta, and is relatively inaccessible by road except during the dry season. Like most villages in the active portion of the Bengal delta, Govindapur is dispersed in settlement pattern. Houses are built along the raised banks of streams which criss-cross the countryside. Much of the land inside the inhabited area of the village is low-lying, filled with marsh grasses, bamboo, patches of jungle, and tanks from which earth has been removed for raising house platforms.

Most Govindapur families depend primarily upon agriculture for their livelihoods. Outside the inhabited area of the village virtually all land is employed in the cultivation of a single wet rice crop each year. A few plots which are near tanks may be used during the dry season to grow potatoes, pulses, or other minor crops. For almost twenty years now, however, most people in the Govindapur area have been engaged in the commercial cultivation of betel leaf, which involves only small plots of land, utilizes labor intensively, and brings a substantial cash income. The deltaic silt of the area is ideally suited to the cultivation of this leaf. Extremely high population density (over 1,500 persons per square mile) means that plots of rice land large enough to feed a family are scarce and very expensive.

The village had a population of 677 in 1960. There are representatives of eleven different castes in Govindapur, an unusually large number for a village in this area (see Nicholas & Mukhopadhyay, 1965), but most people (423 or 63 per cent) are members of the Mahisya cultivator caste. Households of this group held two-thirds (156 acres) of all land owned by Govindapur residents. The Mahisyas stand high in the local system of caste ranking, constitute a majority in virtually all the villages of Midnapore District, and otherwise qualify as the dominant caste of the village and the area. The only other castes which have substantial populations in Govindapur are the Potters (21 households, 86 persons owning 9 per cent of the land), Herdsmen (5 households, 32 persons owning 8 per cent of the land), and Brahmans (6 households, 30 persons owning 9 per cent of the land). Only the Herdsmen and Potters figure importantly *as caste groups* in Govindapur politics; political affairs in the village, on the whole, are *not* caste affairs.

Fifty years of social conflict in Govindapur
About 1910 the fathers of many of the present leaders of Govindapur figured prominently in village affairs. The two leading rivals at that time were Siva Mukhya,[5] father of Hari the present headman, and Niranjan, father of a current oppositionist and village schoolmaster, Ram. Siva Mukhya built his center of influence largely on the east side of the canal which passes through the village; Niranjan held much property and had most supporters on the west side. About 1913, simultaneously it seems, Siva and Niranjan determined to construct temples. To construct a temple is meritorious and confers prestige upon the builder. Also, agricultural land attached to a temple as *devottar* property was not taxed, and a crafty owner could hold a good deal of land tax-free in this way. Siva Mukhya dedicated his temple to *Raghunāth*; he signed over about 100 acres of revenue-producing land and about thirty acres of share-cropped land to

31

the deity. He continued to administer the land himself, however, and brought a Brahman family to live near the temple and perform daily worship there.

Niranjan dedicated his temple to two representations of *Kṛṣṇa*, *Śrīdhar Gopāl* and *Śyām Sundar*. Though not so wealthy as Siva Mukhya, he gave land producing an annual revenue of Rs. 400 plus about ten acres of rice and raised garden land to the deities. In 1915 he handed over the affairs of the temple to a North Indian Brahman. The Brahman served the temple for about two years, then left for another part of the District taking the deeds to the temple property with him. About 1920 a Bihari *sādhu* named Krisnadas Mahanta, who was living in a nearby village, offered to take charge of the temple and recover the land. In fact, Niranjan had by then recovered the land through a technicality, but if Krisnadas Mahanta could induce the Brahman to relinquish his claim an expensive court session might be avoided. Therefore, Niranjan agreed and, eventually, Krisnadas was successful. Krisnadas became priest of the temple, but continued to live in another village, employing a Govinda-pur Brahman to perform daily worship in the temple. He believed he had control over the lands of the temple and apparently shared the proceeds amicably with Niranjan. Krisnadas inherited the property of a temple in the village where he lived and, in his aggressive style, soon began to diversify his economic operations to include lending money to cultivators. Because of his connection with Govindapur, many of his borrowers were residents of this village.

In 1940 Siva Mukhya died and his family suffered a temporary setback. Siva was twice married and father of twelve children. There was a distinct cleavage between the children of the two wives, probably related to the dissatisfaction of the second wife that her own eldest son would not succeed to the headmanship, and that her daughters had been married in other villages while the first wife's daughters were married to sons of important Govindapur families. When Hari became head of the family, his youngest half-brother, Nitai, decided to sell his share of the family property and move to an area where uncultivated land was available. The remaining three half-brothers decided that they too would partition the joint property. Had joint property been maintained – as Hari would have liked – the family would stand far above all others in economic power; with partition, there were four (later five, when Nitai returned to Govindapur) moderately well-to-do families. And Hari, a younger and less wealthy man than Niranjan, was confronted with the problem of consolidating political power over the village.

Siva Mukhya had extended his influence in the portion of the village west of the canal through a series of marriages. His two eldest daughters were married to sons of two large, prosperous families in that neighborhood. A third wealthy family was allied to Siva's when his youngest son, Nitai, was married to a daughter from that group. In Bengal, as in much of North India, the relation between a man and his wife's brother is formally distant and frequently hostile. (In Bengali the most common term of abuse is *śālā*, 'wife's brother'.) All three of these alliances turned to ashes in the hands of Hari when he succeeded to the headmanship, and these three families constituted the core of the anti-headman group among the Mahisya caste in 1960 Govindapur politics. To be sure, the rivalry between Hari Mukhya and his sisters' husbands was not merely an institutionalized kin conflict; after the division of Siva's property among five sons, political and economic rivalry between these families became a much more realistic possibility.

Faced with both the opposition of Niranjan's family and the formidable group of sisters' affines, Hari was anxious to gather support in whatever ways he could. Of course, his share-croppers were supporters, as were the men who cultivated the *devottar* property of the common village temples – Hari personally collected 50 per cent of the produce of this land, in the name of the village, and paid the priests himself. He regularly employed the low-caste Toddy-tappers and several poor Mahisya men who lived near him as agricultural laborers, and he loaned several of them small amounts of money. He could count on their physical support, but poor men had no influence in village decision-making or in the settling of disputes. He needed not so much supporters as allies, and he needed them on the populous west side of the canal. He had to look for persons outside the principal families, and one of the first persons to whom he turned was Krisnadas Mahanta.

Krisnadas was still living in a nearby village and lending money in Govindapur and other areas. In 1950 he moved into Niranjan's temple and began to use it as a center of operations. During the next three years relations between Krisnadas and Niranjan became increasingly hostile, and Krisnadas became increasingly friendly with Hari Mukhya. In 1953 Niranjan and Krisnadas fought physically. Krisnadas left the temple to live in the house of a man named Arjun, an ally of the headman. Krisnadas still believed that he held title to the land attached to Niranjan's temple and appointed a village Brahman to perform worship there. During the next two years he was occupied in constructing a large, expensive temple dedicated to *Sitā* and *Rām* on a plot of land slightly outside the inhabited area of the village. In 1955 he moved into his new temple with his servant woman, a young Mahisya widow named Kalpana, and his disciple, a young Brahman from the family which served Hari Mukhya's temple.

In the meantime, old Niranjan died. His eldest son had preceded him, so the second son, Ram, who was intended to be a schoolmaster, became head of the household. Ram's political position was weakened by joint family difficulties, as Hari Mukhya's had been fifteen years previous. Niranjan had maintained a joint family with his younger brother. The younger brother decided to partition the joint property and shortly thereafter began to suffer from asthma and heart disease; his fortunes declined as Niranjan's rose and his son, Kali, came into bitter conflict with Niranjan and later Ram over the property. When Ram discovered that his father had long ago recovered title to the family temple lands, he expelled Krisnadas' appointee and named a Brahman from another village to serve the temple. Kali lodged an unsuccessful claim to some of the proceeds from the temple lands.

Krisnadas Mahanta's affairs in the new Sita Ram temple were not going altogether smoothly either. He was a wealthy and successful man, but he was now quite old. Consequently, the young Brahman disciple had no difficulty in alienating the affections of Kalpana, the Mahanta's servant woman. Krisnadas promised Kalpana that he would leave her some land on his death if she remained with him in his declining years, and she agreed. The Brahman – to Hari Mukhya the obvious heir to the Mahanta and thus, potentially, an important and easily influenced ally – remained too, but kept his distance from Krisnadas. One day, only about a year before the old Mahanta's death, a young Bihari police officer came to visit him, having heard that there was a fellow Bihari in the area. The police officer, named Ramdas, flattered the old man, who then convinced him of the moral and material benefits of life as a Mahanta. Ramdas thus became Krisnadas' second disciple and, when he died, heir to a considerable fortune. The young Brahman was disowned despite Hari Mukhya's support.

Krisnadas died suddenly while Ramdas was away in another part of the District. It is widely believed that Hari Mukhya and Kalpana immediately seized several thousand rupees in cash which was hidden in the temple. Kalpana took the titles to the land which was promised her and went to live with the young Brahman and his family. Ramdas was in a rage when he discovered what had happened and subsequently spent much time and effort trying to reclaim both the money and the land. In pursuit of his claim against the headman, Ramdas was a natural ally of the opposition.

Hari Mukhya was himself still searching for allies to strengthen his position in the increasingly hostile west side of the village. He proved a very useful intermediary for men 'on their way up' in the world. A man who was rising economically inevitably had to fight many cases in government courts, pursuing tenuous claims to land, hoping weak opponents would give up easily rather than risk financial ruin in the courts. Hari Mukhya was a valuable ally for such a man because of his intimacy with the government bureaucracy. Among other positions, he was Union Welfare Officer, which meant he had control over distribution of money and food to the destitute of nine villages. In addition, he had arranged for his son to become tax collector for the Union. These positions gave Hari considerable power over some villagers as well as useful connections with the local government bureaucracy.

Arjun, the man with whom Krisnadas Mahanta lived after his fight with Niranjan, was one of the economically mobile villagers who found the headman's assistance valuable. Arjun began as a servant in the house of oppositionist Krisna's father. He eventually established a claim to some of the land on which he had worked and, using his first property skilfully, had become a prosperous cultivator of eight acres by 1960. Much of his land came from Krisna's family and, though he continued to live in their midst, the breach was never healed. This made him a natural ally of the headman, but as a lone figure without a large kin group, without share-croppers (he and his brother parsimoniously cultivated the eight acres themselves), he was not of much use to Hari.

Visnu was another man who pursued his fortune aggressively. His father was a moderately prosperous cultivator who left him about five acres of land. This Visnu immediately parcelled out to share-croppers, and he began to spend most of his time around the courts. He soon developed a special style of operation: he entered land litigation on behalf of the weaker claimant, bought the disputed plot from him at a low price, and fought the case in court himself. Several pleaders in town were obligated to Visnu for 'touting' or directing clients to them. Many friends in and around the courts helped him when he pursued a case of his own. Until about 1955 Visnu operated as a 'lone wolf' in village affairs; then he came into direct conflict with opposition leader Chandi, his nearest neighbor. Visnu had previously been close to Niranjan's faction, but its strength and importance seemed to be declining at the time, and also it was connected with Chandi's faction. He turned to Hari Mukhya, who was only too happy to have an aggressive, wealthy ally like Visnu on his weak western flank. Visnu found Hari's connection with the government bureaucracy valuable also. By 1960 Visnu had amassed over eleven acres of land and was in pursuit of more. This land was cultivated by fifteen men of different families, twelve in Govindapur and three in the neighboring village of Radhanagar. Visnu was 'tough' and demanded unquestioning loyalty from his share-croppers.

The events related thus far have concerned almost exclusively the Mahisya caste. Some of the sustained conflicts in Govindapur have concerned minority castes also. Old Siva Mukhya did not bother the Govindapur Potter caste group a great deal. Until about 1920, when a group of outsiders moved in, all the Potters in Govindapur were descendants of a single man and they ran affairs in their neighborhood very much as a large extended family might. Several events which occurred after 1943 brought the Potters increasingly into village affairs. When Hari became headman one of the methods he employed to extend his control in the village was 'subordination'. If he intervened in small local disputes – which he might easily do in the neighborhoods of poor minority castes – and brought about a settlement, he might supersede the less powerful senior men in the locality In this way he gained control over the low-ranking Toddy-tappers and in the mixed-caste neighborhood near his house, but many of these people were economically dependent upon him and thus under some pressure to accept his decisions anyway. The Potters lived in the politically important west side of the village and Hari determined to exert his authority over them. The Potters were acutely conscious of their inferior caste position in a Mahisya-dominated society, so when Hari Mukhya attempted to interfere in a dispute they rallied around their own headman, Durga Potter, against the outsider. But a new generation was succeeding the old one, and as the distance between the Potters and their common ancestor increased, so did the social distance between the various descent groups. One such group, headed by Suren Potter, was under heavy criticism because one of its members, Tapan, was 'behaving like a Mahisya': he was attempting to seize land by foreclosing in usufructuary mortgages. During the height of the tension, Suren arranged the marriage of his son without consulting the Potter headman or other members of the group. In the ensuing dispute Suren's descent group supported his action and the entire group was boycotted. Hari Mukhya supported Suren's group, in return for which they now support him in village affairs, as do the unrelated Potters.

The Govindapur Herdsman caste group was smaller and less closely tied by kinship and co-residence, but more prosperous than the Potters. The group was, however, unified and watchful of its interests under the vigorous leadership of seventy-year-old Rakhal Herdsman. Rakhal was head of the eastern Midnapore Herdsman caste organization. Like the Potters, the Herdsmen generally in Bengal rank higher than the Mahisyas but must

37

accept their dominance in Midnapore. Rakhal and his group have always trod a cautious middle ground in village politics. Kanai, an aggressive and intelligent young man from one Herdsman household, allied himself with Hari Mukhya. Bhima, head of a large Herdsman joint family, was just as closely allied with the opposition. Kanai lives near the canal and thus near the headman's house; Bhima's nearest neighbors are oppositionists. Between these two families lives Rakhal whose stance in village affairs – like his residence – is squarely in the center. He associates with both groups and gets on equally well with Hari Mukhya and opposition leader Chandi.

The panchayat election

The election of members to the *grām panchayat* (village council) which was held in Govindapur in the autumn of 1959 brought about what I shall call, with thanks to Hugh Gray, a 'crystallization' of political alignments in the village. Political leaders canvassed villagers for support; they utilized every possible tie to bring out votes. Leaders discussed among themselves, organized coalitions, and jockeyed for position. During the pre-election period almost all relations of alliance and opposition between villagers became clear, and it is these relations which were reported to me at the end of 1960.

Under the Indian government scheme for the 'decentralization of administration' each revenue village was to elect a council with a number of members in proportion to its population. Each village panchayat was to send up one delegate, not a member of the panchayat, to the *anchal* or area panchayat which covered a group of fifteen to twenty villages. Eventually, power to levy and collect taxes for use in local development work was to be given to anchal panchayats. In preparation for the first panchayat election in Govindapur, an official from the Block Development Office responsible for the village visited Hari Mukhya and together they divided the village into two consituencies. The east side of the canal was joined with the northernmost portion of the village on the west side to make a constituency 'safe' for the headman's supporters. The opposition groups were almost entirely confined to the south constituency,

38

where it was hoped they might defeat one another in triangular contests.

Workers from both Congress and Communist parties, who had canvassed the village during two national general elections, came to prepare their supporters for the panchayat election also. Hari Mukhya, like most village headmen in West Bengal, was strongly identified with the Congress party; this identification left the opposition little choice – they were Communists or nothing. The rearrangement of political conflict along partisan lines brought home to the opposition leaders the necessity of coalition. There were five distinct opposition factions in the village at the time of the election, but none of them, alone, could muster a quarter of the voting strength commanded by Hari Mukhya. If each of these factions, or even two or three of them, offered its own slate of candidates, they all stood a very good chance of defeat.

Chandi and his matrilateral cross-cousin Krisna, with a comparatively large factional following, were joined by Ramdas Mahanta, who lacked followers but was wealthy and well-educated. Ramdas prevailed upon his friend Durga Potter who brought the large Potter vote-bloc into the coalition. Gopal, undisputed 'boss' of the isolated neighborhood on the extreme west side of the village, was unenthusiastic about the Communist party but willingly joined an alliance with his friends Chandi and Krisna against his wife's brother, Hari Mukhya. Govinda, the only prosperous cultivator outside the headman's kin group on the east side of the canal, also lent his small support to the coalition.

The alliance within the opposition structured very strongly the choices of Ram and Visnu. Ram and Ramdas Mahanta carried on the fight over the property of Ram's family temple. Ram saw that the Mahanta, without any political following, was being given a position of importance in the coalition. His struggle for precedence over the headman's family went on, and he would certainly vote against Hari Mukhya, but he could not join an alliance with Ramdas Mahanta. The opposition leaders regarded Ram's family as a declining force in the village, since it was internally divided and much less wealthy than it had been. Visnu had little choice, both because of his attachment to the headman and because of his bitter conflict with Chandi. Although Visnu's house was in the midst of the opposition neighborhood, his share-croppers were located throughout the village. Facing a losing battle against the united opposition in his own locality, he could still bring out a number of important votes in the northern constituency.

Rakhal Herdsman went about the village in his usual way agreeing with everyone about what needed to be done. Young Kanai Herdsman, however, cultivated Hari Mukhya's friendship assiduously during the pre-election period. Bhima Herdsman was close to Gopal and promised the support of his family to the opposition. (When the election actually came, Rakhal voted Congress and his wife voted Communist – at least, that is what Rakhal told other villagers.)

The Congress and Communist coalitions each fielded four candidates, two from each of the constituencies, plus a candidate for the anchal panchayat to be elected by the new panchayat members. Since the candidate for the anchal could not be a member of the village panchayat, each group had to hold in reserve one strong candidate.

	Congress candidates	*Communist candidates*
North constituency	Kali*	Nitai
	Kanai Herdsman*	Syama
South constituency	Visnu	Krisna*
	Arjun	Durga Potter*
Anchal panchayat	Hari Mukhya*	Chandi

* = successful candidates

The choice of candidates by the two coalitions reflects some careful political calculation. The north constituency was predominantly under Hari Mukhya's control; the Congress candidates chosen were the ones who stood the greatest chance of winning marginal votes. Kali, Ram's disaffected classificatory brother, might win votes from his kinsmen, and Kanai Herdsman might ensure the support of his caste group. The opposition chose Hari Mukhya's half-brother Nitai in hopes of dividing the headman's kin group. Syama was a moderately prosperous grocer who lived just inside the north constituency boundary, well away from the headman's sphere of influence, which made him slightly stronger than Govinda, the other possible candidate.

The south constituency proved to be as 'safe' for the opposition as the north was for the Congress. Neither Krisna nor Durga Potter was a particularly wealthy or powerful leader. Krisna had a large kin group while Durga had the large group of loyal Potters. Much more important was that the combined forces of Chandi, Ramdas Mahanta, and Gopal were behind them. Thus, though they were opposed by two wealthy and powerful candidates, Visnu and Arjun, both won easily.

The two most powerful candidates, Hari Mukhya and Chandi, were held in reserve for the anchal panchayat election. Of course, with two votes for Chandi and two for the headman, the choice of an anchal member was at first a standoff. Ultimately, Krisna and Durga Potter had to admit that it would not be proper for the village to send someone other than the headman to the anchal panchayat, so they agreed to elect Hari Mukhya.

It is not surprising that the men who, despite the election, continue to carry the most weight in the village, to make most of the decisions, or to prevent one another from making them, are Hari Mukhya, Visnu, and Chandi – none of them a member of the village panchayat. In practice, a panchayat meeting is still what it was before the election, a loose congregation of important men who gather whenever a village decision must be taken, a dispute settled, or a case decided and punishment meted out. Most of the affairs with which they deal are not the officially defined business of a village panchayat and, indeed, they do not pay much attention to their official business. Still, the election was seen as an important event which tested the strength of village factions. Further, villagers have been told that bursary functions will one day be handed over to panchayats, and no one wants to let funds be controlled by his enemies, since they would certainly be used to alienate his political followers.

Recruitment to factions

Throughout this account I have attempted to tell, wherever the question arose, what kind of link connected a faction leader and a follower. In *Table 1* I set down systematically the connections of adult villagers to faction leaders. This tabulation reflects information given primarily by Hari Mukhya, Chandi, Krisna, Durga Potter, and Visnu's nephew. Connections are not always

TABLE 1

Factional alignments of all possible voters in Govindapur[a]

Faction leader	Party	Possible voters supporting by basis of support					
		Kinship	Factors related to caste	Economic dependence	Leader is neighborhood headman	Leader opposes mutual enemy	Total
Hari Mukhya	Congress	13	12	57	18	26	126
Visnu	Congress	9	–	16	13	3	41
Rakhal Herdsman	Independent (pro-Congress)	3	12	–	9	–	24
Ram	Independent (pro-Communist)	7	–	5	–	–	12[c]
Chandi & Krisna	Communist	24	–	4	8	–	36
Durga Potter	Communist	7	24	–	–	–	31
Gopal	Communist	17	–	1	11	–	29
Govinda	Communist	14	–	–	3	2	19
Ramdas Mahanta	Communist	1	–	5	–	–	6
		95	48	88	62	31	324

[a] Data included in *Table 2* of Nicholas and Mukhopadhyay 1965 have here been re-analyzed to show possible voters rather than only households. By 'possible voters' is meant members of village households whose ages were reported to me as 21 years or above; this does not tell how many persons were registered as voters. Votes from faction leaders' own households are included in the category 'kinship'.

[b] Includes 17 Congress and 7 Communist votes.

[c] Includes 10 Communist and 2 Congress votes.

clear and occasionally they are multiple, as in the case of some of Chandi's share-croppers who are also relatives; the relation between them is observably one of 'affection' rather than 'subordination'. In this case I have charged half the votes to kinship and half to economic dependence, though the kin connection may be the primary tie between them.

I identified factions initially by villagers' references to *dal*, a word which in local usage means 'faction', 'party' (but not a political party), 'group', or 'band'. The term is used to describe a group of traveling performers, a band of men who sing devotional songs, drinking companions, and village political factions. A political faction can be distinguished from other kinds of *dal* by the fact that the leader uses the expression 'I have a number of men in my hand'. Only faction leaders use such an expression, and other villagers may describe them as having such a group. If asked, Govindapur faction leaders may enumerate the adult men they could muster in a fight, though they usually exaggerate. Actual physical conflicts, known to the villagers as *mārāmāri* ('a beating affair'), are comparatively rare, but 'factional affairs' (*dalādali*) are not at all uncommon.

The most ordinary sort of conflict in the village, however, is *gālāgāli*, 'a shouting affair'. One man's bullock strays into another man's garden and eats some plants; the garden owner beats the bullock and drives him out. The bullock's owner abuses his neighbor for beating the animal. The mutual recriminations develop in intensity as they go on, and the first prominent man to hear the dispute is expected to appear and settle it. The only essential qualification for such a referee is that he should have some authority – i.e. he should be relatively wealthy – and that he should live within shouting distance of the disputants. In a dispersed village like Govindapur, authority for settling *gālāgāli* disputes must also be dispersed. (In general usage, the village is divided into four wards, each with its own leaders.) Authority expressed in this way, though it appears not to amount to a great deal, proved to be important for political recruitment in Govindapur. In the table it is seen that 62 votes were decided by the influence of the neighborhood headman, either because there was an element of subordination in their relationship, because the headman had recently decided disputes in favor of his supporter's household, or because the supporter hoped to win favor. Offended parties, however, were likely to support an opposed faction. Hari Mukhya collected the votes of several households which felt they had been wronged in one dispute or another.

Analysis

If I were to analyze the case just presented *in vacuo* I would doubtless be able to derive from it the five criteria which I believe define 'faction'. I might at the same time erroneously decide that factions almost always persist over comparatively long periods of time, that this variety of factional activity is peculiar to peasant societies, or that some other inessential characteristic is fundamental. By framing beforehand a set of criteria, based upon a wide-ranging comparison of related social phenomena, I am able, figuratively speaking, to 'read' the events in Govindapur directly in sociological terms. Posterior analysis is undoubtedly most productive of coherent structures; it is less useful, however, in getting a grasp of 'dynamic phenomena'. I shall briefly recapitulate the elements in the definition to see what light they shed on Govindapur politics.

1. Factions are conflict groups. There was a great deal of obvious conflict in the village both prior to and during the panchayat election. Factions appeared as groups (or, perhaps better, as quasi-groups) only during conflict. But, curiously, there are several instances of factions cooperating with one another, of factional 'coalitions' or 'alliances'. If the criterion of conflict is observed, there seems to be no way of accomodating alliances. Looked at over time, however, factions may be seen moving from alliance to opposition; factions do not lose their separate identities in an alliance. This objection will be dealt with further under Item 4 below.

2. Factions are political groups. In citing a definition of politics, I directed attention to 'the use of public power'. Following Bailey (1960, p. 10), I conceive of power as command over resources and control over men. Analyzing politics in a small society, it is not always clear how much socially recognized power is to be thought of as 'public' and how much as 'private'. Commonly owned resources, such as the land attached to the Govindapur village temples, certainly belong to the public arena; the headman had command over this resource and, thereby, control over the men who utilized it. The governments of the Indian Union and the State of West Bengal have intervened in the village to define an area of public power – the business of the new panchayat – and the means by which that power should be disposed – universal adult franchise election. Given this definition of the situation, Govindapur political leaders immediately converted their 'private power', such as control over share-croppers, debtors, kinsmen, neighbors, etc., into public, political power in the form of votes.

3. Factions are not corporate groups. A student of tribal societies examining an Indian peasant community might reasonably expect to find that the obvious corporate segments of the society, castes, would provide the structure for village political relations as they do for economic relations. Although two minority caste groups in Govindapur, Potters and Herdsmen, appear as more or less united political groups, description of inter-caste conflict would not come close to describing Govindapur politics. Analyzing caste in purely abstract, structural terms, Bailey (1963, p. 118) points out that the system, ideally, permits only cooperative and never competitive relations between castes. 'Only the dominant caste has an autonomous political existence, not as a corporate political group, but as a field for political competition. Certainly no subordinate caste is a corporate political group.' Within the dominant Mahisya caste of Govindapur there is no single principle which organizes political relations. Among certain Jat and Thakur dominant caste groups in some North Indian villages, as in the case of Rampur described by Lewis (1958), segments of a unilineal descent group or clans may organize political conflict (see Note 2, p. 59). In Govindapur, however, no such divisions are reckoned within the dominant caste and, to a great extent, it is 'every man for himself' in village politics.

4. Faction members are recruited by a leader. The essential position of the leader in organizing a Govindapur faction is obvious without further analysis here; there is neither structural principle nor common interest to hold together faction members in the absence of the leader. Certain factions, particularly those based upon large extended kinship groups, may have 'clique' leadership like that described by Beals (1959, p. 433). The faction based among some west ward Mahisya families and led by Chandi and Krisna is an example of clique leadership. To return to the question of factional coalitions mentioned above, it was

Ralph W. Nicholas

seen that separate factions continue to be distinct from one
another even when they are in alliance. The fundamental reason
for this is that two faction leaders can never have identical
interests; with resources as scarce as they are in Govindapur,
men powerful enough to be faction leaders are always at least
potentially in conflict.

5. Faction members are recruited on diverse principles. An analysis
of the bases upon which Govindapur voters supported their
faction leaders during the 1960 panchayat election shows that
29 per cent were kinsmen and 27 per cent were economic dependents of their leaders; 19 per cent of the voters backed their
neighborhood headman, 15 per cent gave their support on
grounds related to caste, and 10 per cent endorsed leaders in
hopes of defeating a mutual enemy. In other villages, grounds
for support might appear to be dramatically different, but they
are invariably diverse (cf. Benedict, 1957, p. 340).

III. FACTIONS AND POLITICAL CHANGE

In the preceding sections which define faction and analyzed the
social organization of factions in a concrete instance, the question of 'origin' was studiously avoided. Obviously there are cases
in which the genesis of factions is recorded and may be sociologically analyzed without recourse to conjectural history. The
persistent connection of factionalism with social change suggests
that, in at least one context, it may be possible to discuss this
political process in greater time depth than is permitted by
functional analysis.

Where communities, like the Fiji Indian village discussed in
Section I, have been deprived of political authority, factions
seem to arise unbidden to organize the personnel in disputes.
Siegel and Beals (1960, p. 399) assert that factionalism of the
kind described in the preceding pages 'is essentially a phenomenon of socio-cultural change'. And as a definition they offer:
'Factionalism is overt conflict in a group which leads to increasing abandonment of cooperative activities'. This definition
suggests that factions may eventually 'work themselves out'

46

when all cooperative activity in a community has been abandoned. Such a conclusion does not fit well with the long lifetimes of factions in some societies. With Siegel and Beals, I find factionalism frequently connected with change in political structure, but I think factions, in the absence of conventional political divisions, perform necessary functions in organizing conflict. The example of the Iroquois will help to show what I mean.

Aboriginal Iroquois politics

By careful study of Lewis Henry Morgan's *League of the Iroquois* (1901) and other historical works, and by comparison with better-analyzed segmentary political systems, it is possible to discover a good deal about the pre-contact political system of the Iroquois. They were semi-sedentary cultivators and hunters living in what is now upper New York State. The name 'Iroquois' actually covers five – and later six – tribes which formed a Confederation or League including the Mohawk, Onondaga, Oneida, Seneca, and Cayuga tribes which speak related, mutually unintelligible languages. The sixth tribe, the Tuscaroras, lived in the area of what is now Delaware. Driven out of their homelands by white settlement, they joined the League over a period between 1715 and 1722, but never occupied full status on the Council (Morgan, 1928, p. 16).

According to traditional Iroquois history, the Confederation was founded – perhaps late in the sixteenth century – by one Deganawidah, who is said to have been troubled by strife between the component tribes (Scott *et al.*, 1911). Each of the original five tribes (with minor exceptions) was made up of a series of like-named matriclans. The brotherhood of fellow clansmen in different tribes seems to have been an important cross-tying principle in what was otherwise a loose political alliance (Morgan, 1901, I, pp. 77-78). The clans were divided into two ritually and socially opposed moieties. Members of opposite moieties (called by Morgan 'phratries') occupied the two ends of the 'Longhouse' in which ceremonies were held. All of the gambling and athletic events in Iroquois life symbolized one of the levels of social segmentation. As Morgan (1901, I, p. 281) wrote:

'They were strifes between nation and nation [i.e. tribes], village and village, or tribes and tribes [i.e. clans]; in a word, parties against parties, and not champion against champion. The prize contended for was that of victory; and it belonged, not to triumphant players, but to the party which sent them forth to the contest.'

Morgan (1881, pp. 12-14) noted other functions of Iroquois dual divisions. When a murderer and his victim were of opposite moieties, a moiety council would be called and negotiations for reparation would be conducted between the moieties. If both murderer and victim were members of the same division, discussion would be carried on by representatives of their respective clans. At the funeral of a particularly important person the body would be addressed by members of the opposite moiety. The body would then be carried to the grave by members of the opposite moiety followed, in order, by the family of the deceased, members of his clan, other clans of his moiety, and finally members of the opposite moiety. The directly political functions of Iroquois dual divisions are best seen in the fact that the appointment of a new chief had to be approved first by his own moiety – which rarely objected – then by the opposite moiety – which rarely failed to object to an appointment.

Morgan could not be expected to see that Iroquois clans were composed of a number of matrilineages, one or occasionally two of which were politically dominant and responsible for the appointment of chiefs. He did notice, however, that a new chief was frequently 'a son of one of the deceased ruler's sisters' or 'one of his brothers' (Morgan, 1901, I, p. 84). Goldenweiser (1915, pp. 366-367) said the power to name a chief resided with the senior woman of what he called the 'maternal family'. Recent research by Merlin Myers has revealed that Goldenweiser's 'maternal family' is, in fact, a corporate matrilineage. Morgan (1901, I, pp. 60-61) identified fifty named chiefships ('sachem-ships') which composed the Council of the Confederacy. They admitted to their discussions some 'Pinetree Chiefs', men who had distinguished themselves as leaders without being appointed to named chiefships. Such positions died with their holders. The Council dealt, of course, only with affairs of common concern, and local matters were handled by the chiefs of each tribe or clan. Tribes occupied their own territories and land seems to have been held by the clan under the primary control of the dominant lineage.

Early contact political cleavages
The nice balance of equal, opposed, 'nesting' social segments was disturbed early in the eighteenth century by a cleavage within the League between supporters of the English and supporters of the French in North America (Fenton, 1955, p. 338). Partisans of the French, many of them Mohawks, but members of other tribes also, were converted to Roman Catholicism and led to new settlements in Quebec by Jesuit missionaries. The second major schism in the League was created by the American Revolution, some members of all tribes supporting the British and others the colonists.

In 1784 Frederick Haldimand, Governor of Quebec and its adjacent territories, signed a deed giving to the Mohawk Indians and 'others of the Six Nations who have either lost their settlement within the territory of the American States, or wish to retire from them to the British', a strip of land six miles wide on either side of the Grand River from the source to the mouth. Joseph Brant, a Mohawk Pinetree Chief, had sought and won this grant in order to bring the tribes of the Confederacy into one area, thereby preventing the complete dissolution of the alliance and loss of its political and military power. Many of the Iroquois who had fought on the side of the colonists or been neutrals remained in New York. Some of the Mohawks who had fought on the British side had already taken up new territory along the Bay of Quinte on a strip of land granted by the British shortly after the conclusion of the Revolution. The Senecas were urging other member tribes to move into the Genesee valley where they held land. The League was losing its unity and power. When Brant pulled together the remnants of the Six Nations on the Grand River Reserve it was apparently with an eye to salvaging whatever bargaining power he still had with the British. With members of all six tribes of the Confederacy living within the confines of a single reserved area, functions of local government seem to have gone automatically into the hands

D   49

of the Council of chiefs. Of the fifty named Iroquois chiefships, thirty-nine remained on the Grand River Reserve at the end of the nineteenth century (Chadwick, 1897, pp. 86-97).

The reservation period

Both of the early schisms in the Iroquois Confederacy, the French vs. British and British vs. colonist, cut across all six tribes. There is no way of knowing the structural bases of these divisions, so it is not possible to tell if they were fundamentally factional. Something is known, however, about a religious cleavage which became apparent in Iroquois society during the nineteenth century. Many supporters of the British cause were or became Protestant Christians, largely Anglicans. The group which migrated to the Grand River Reserve included both Christians and followers of traditional Iroquois religion. Early in the nineteenth century a Seneca preacher named Handsome Lake began to propagate a syncretic revivalist religion known as the 'Good Message'. It was quickly accepted by the non-Christians in both the United States and Canada, but it was not successful in the reconversion of the Christians (Noon, 1949, p. 19). The faith taught by Handsome Lake is still an integral part of the aboriginal social system wherever it is found, and is generally known as the 'Longhouse Religion', since followers carry on their ceremonies in traditional long wooden buildings which were, in origin, lineage dwellings. The vigor of the Longhouse revival apparently deepened the religious schism, so that by Morgan's time there was a group which he described (1901, II, pp. 112-113) as a 'Christian Party' among the Iroquois in New York. The cleavage between Christians and non-Christians goes very deep, as examination of contemporary factions on the Grand River Reserve will show.

Early in the present century the Canadian government resolved to rid itself of the Indian problem by encouraging the assimilation of Indians. In line with this policy, the government in 1924 eagerly responded to the wishes of a number of Six Nations men who sought to replace the hereditary Council of the League with an elective council. The installation of the elective council divided the people, already split along religious lines, into factions according to their support for or opposition to the elective system. This cleavage has persisted to the present, so that the two basic issues of religion and representation provide the basic political divisions on the Six Nations Reserve today.

Contemporary factional politics
In March 1959, the hereditary chiefs of the Six Nations, supported by several hundred young men, marched into the old council house and forcibly expelled the elective council. They issued a proclamation declaring themselves the legal government of the 'independent Indian nation of Grand River'. In 1924 many of the same hereditary chiefs had themselves been ejected from the council house by Royal Canadian Mounted Police who had been dispatched by the government to support the elective council. By the end of March the hereditary chiefs had again been evicted from the council house by the R.C.M.P., but they continued to hold meetings as they always had, and to receive at least passive support from a majority of the Reserve's 6,385 inhabitants. Behind this incident lies a complex of political action based ostensibly upon the cleavages created by religion and by views on election as a method of selecting a government. These two cross-cutting cleavages gave four principal factions on the Reserve when I studied it in 1958.

(i) *The 'Progressive' faction.* The men who originally petitioned the Canadian government to displace the Council of the League with an elective council form the basis of the 'progressive'[6] group. Since 1924 they have attracted many ambitious young men into their camp. All members of this group are Christians and many of them are among the hardest-working and most prosperous farmers. They have ambitions for large houses and automobiles, and encourage their children to continue their education off the Reserve. They often comment unfavorably on the behavior of the Longhouse people. They attempt to maintain white friends and occasionally encourage their children to marry whites.

The Progressive faction depicts the hereditary council as 'primitive' and 'unprogressive'; something which, like the Longhouse religion, gives Indians low social status in white eyes. Underlying the views of the leaders of this faction, however,

51

seems to be the fact that, to my knowledge, none of them is a member of a chiefly lineage. In other words, the political aspirations of socially successful and economically mobile individuals had, before 1924, been frustrated by hereditary government. For the Progressives there was no course to political power other than changing the system.

(ii) *The Longhouse faction.* It is somewhat misleading to speak of the followers of the Longhouse religion as a 'faction', since they constitute a social group for purposes other than politics. Since this group functions as a faction in relation to other Reserve factions, however, I feel justified in treating it as such. It is significant, moreover, that there are four Longhouses on the Reserve; these are culturally distinct, originally meeting the needs of different tribes, and one of the key aspects of their recent association with one another has been political. Members of all Longhouses may go to hear a visiting preacher in one Longhouse, but their annual ceremonies are separate. The four Longhouses at Grand River are the Sour Spring or Upper Cayuga, Seneca, Onondaga, and Lower Cayuga. The Lower Cayuga Longhouse is, politically, a special case and will be treated separately below.

In 1954 there were 1,260 followers of the Longhouse religion on the Reserve, that is, about 20 per cent of the total population. They did not oppose 'progress' in principle; they were quite willing to take advantage of tractors, power tools, automobiles, and automatic appliances. On the whole, however, they were not prosperous and did not encourage their children to seek much education. Many Longhouse children attended only elementary school, which was offered on the Reserve by Indian teachers. The Longhouse people were localized in the southeast quarter of the Reserve, and the few Christians resident in the area were socially isolated.

The Longhouse group held a majority on the hereditary council, partially because they retained to a greater extent than other groups the recollection of the lineage. The investiture of a chief was a Longhouse ceremony and the naming of a new chief required action on the part of a lineage matron, the eldest female of a chiefly lineage, action less likely to be taken by a

Christian than a Longhouse woman. Since the Canadian government deprived the hereditary council of its right to decide on the economic and civil affairs of the Reserve, this group has had fewer functions. Yet it continued to hold regular meetings and to take decisions which were widely respected on the Reserve. One of the most important decisions of the traditional council was its interdiction of voting in elections. The chiefs said in 1924 that election was not a suitable means for Indians to select a government. Consequently, most people on the Reserve have never voted for members of the elective council.

(iii) *The Lower Cayuga Longhouse.* In 1957, to the surprise of all the factions, members of the Lower Cayuga Longhouse voted in the council election. There are, of course, sound reasons for this unexpected behavior. The Lower Cayugas had recently come under strong criticism from other Longhouses for 'not picking their chiefs correctly', that is, for either not knowing or failing to follow the order of succession in the matrilineage correctly. They betrayed certain 'modernist' tendencies and had even discussed wiring their Longhouse for electricity. Equally important seems to be the fact that, by their united action, the Lower Cayuga group actually elected the chief councilor in 1957.

There were several competitors for the office of chief councilor, all but one of them important figures in the Progressive faction. One elderly man with poor control over English, little education, and little evidence of prosperity was elected, it is said, by the united vote of the Lower Cayuga group. Too many candidates stood for the election and so divided the small number of voters that the comparatively small bloc vote of the Lower Cayuga Longhouse was sufficient to elect the chief councilor. Members of the Lower Cayuga group refer to the chief councilor as 'more of an Indian than most Christians'.

While the Lower Cayuga Longhouse is declining in prestige among the Longhouse people, it has become an important factor in the politics of the Reserve as a whole. Apparently the group made a straightforward political calculation and determined that their interest would best be served by rejecting the most important ruling of the hereditary council.

(iv) *The Mohawk Workers*. The 'Mohawk Workers' are not all workers nor wholly Mohawks. Many men from this group have, at one time or another, worked in high steel construction and been members of trade unions. But not all men who had been thus employed were members of this faction. The group was founded at about the time of the 1924 political crisis by non-Longhouse people who opposed the installation of the elective council. In fact, the leadership of the Mohawk Workers is provided by men of Christian families who claim membership in the hereditary council.

In the political rhetoric of Grand River the Progressives placed primary emphasis upon 'progress' while the Mohawk Workers emphasized 'rights'. Every step taken by the Canadian government in Indian affairs was interpreted by the Mohawk Workers with respect to how it affected their rights. They are particularly concerned with the rights stemming from their original land grant, most of which has passed into white hands by a variety of means until all that now remains is an area seven miles wide and ten miles long. 'No Indian,' said the Mohawk Workers, 'has ever had the right to sell the land granted to all of us; and no white man has the right to take Indian land.' They believe that Iroquois land tenure was once communal and that the Grand River lands belonged to all equally. In 1930 a group of Mohawk Workers was sent to London in a vain attempt to get a ruling from parliament on their right to the alienated land.

In the late 1940s the Mohawk Workers sent a delegation to the United Nations in hopes that they might be recognized as an independent nationality by the world body. The issue of independent nationality is important to many Reserve people who are not necessarily members of this faction. Indians have the right to unhampered border crossing between the U.S. and Canada in recognition of the aboriginal absence of this boundary. Preachers of the Good Message frequently perform marriage ceremonies (though such marriages are not legally recognized in Canada), and they believe that their right to do so derives from their independent nationality.

Mohawk Workers frequently refer to members of the elective council as 'traitors' to the Indians. They employ the term 'loyalist council' to distinguish the elected body from the hereditary council. They frequently assert that members of the elective council 'buy all their votes' with 'bribes' of the welfare money, which they administer. In fact, it is very difficult for a supporter of the Mohawk Workers – or for any non-voter – to receive welfare benefits, while recipients have been observed to build new houses while living on welfare funds. In order to teach school on the Reserve an Indian must sign an oath of loyalty to the government of Canada. The Mohawk Workers regard assent to this oath as 'taking a bribe', that is, signing away Indian 'nationality' for the sake of a monthly wage.

It would be a mistake to think of the Mohawk Workers as a clearly structured group. Leadership seems to be diffuse except in crisis situations, when it comes from members of the hereditary council. Thus also, there are stronger and weaker supporters of the faction. The Progressive faction also lacks clear leadership, though a few members of this group who are more prosperous and better educated are treated as spokesmen for the faction. Only the Longhouse people have any kind of formal organization, based upon their recognition of the primacy of the chiefs and lineage matrons, and their affiliation with one or another Longhouse. Any member of Reserve society, however, can easily identify the factional affiliation of any other person, whether he is politically active or not. The two diacritical phenomena, religion and voting or non-voting, can be applied to any member of the society to determine his place in the system of political alignments.

Factions and social change

My principal intention in dealing with factional politics among the Iroquois is to elucidate the relation between factions and social change. American Indian societies, particularly those with aboriginal acephalous political systems, have suffered the most intense external pressure. The fact that so many of these societies, subjected to similar forces, have factioned suggests a regularity, noted over twenty-five years ago by Linton (1936, p. 229):

'Among American Indians the pattern of factions is certainly deep-seated. In some cases two factions have survived for generations, changing leaders and the bases of their disputes and winning some individuals from each other. . . . Opposition seems to be the main reason for their existence, their policies and declared grounds for opposition shifting with the circumstances. In some cases any cause which is espoused by one will immediately be resisted by the other.'

The first band of Iroquois which migrated to Canada after the American Revolution was made up of Christian Mohawks who settled at Tayendenaga on the Bay of Quinte. There was no religious cleavage to provide an initial organizing principle, yet when the Canadian government introduced the elective system on this Reserve, an anti-government faction immediately rose to oppose the change. This group, known as the 'Longhairs' soon began to participate in the elections, however, and about 1958 this faction controlled the Reserve council.

Fenton (1955, p. 338) has reported similar factions among Iroquois on the Tonawanda and Onondaga Reservations in New York, while he says 'true political parties' operate among the New York Senecas. Wallace (1952, p. 33) has described the strong factional tendencies he found among the New York Tuscaroras. At Taos Pueblo in New Mexico (Fenton, 1957, pp. 317-318, 335) there are the out-of-power 'People's Party', which resembles the Mohawk Workers in ideology and action, and the in-power pro-government faction. Fenton (1955, p. 330) has observed similar factions elsewhere in the U.S. among the Klamath and Blackfoot.

Siegel and Beals (1960) are also concerned with the regularity and widespread occurrence of factions. Independently, Siegel observed the factions at Taos, while Beals found a similar pattern in the Indian village of Namhalli described briefly above. They distinguished three varieties of factionalism: party, schismatic, and pervasive factionalism;[7] of these they are primarily concerned with the pervasive form which they assert is common to Taos Pueblo and Namhalli (p. 394), and 'is essentially a phenomenon of socio-cultural change' (p. 399). Such factionalism is the result of 'a complicated interaction between internal strains and external pressures' (p. 414).

The definition of factionalism offered by Siegel and Beals

(p. 399) and discussed at the beginning of this section – 'Factionalism is overt conflict within a group which leads to increasing abandonment of cooperative activities' – is related to the authors' view that 'the main incentive for joining a faction appeared to be hostility toward some members of the opposing faction'. I have attempted here to show that individuals align themselves politically with one another primarily out of self-interest; this interest may in some cases be primarily hostility, but obviously hostility alone cannot explain the factional alignments of all the persons in any political arena. Further, I have attempted to show that factions are conflict groups which perform essential political functions. A factional system is not the political 'state of nature' of any of the societies I have examined. The fact that factions are so often found in rapidly changed or changing societies and institutions has no doubt drawn the attention of Siegel and Beals as well as other observers to the disruptive features of factional politics. If we distinguish between the social disruption brought about by social change and the social order brought about by almost any kind of political system, our attention will be drawn to the functions of factions.

Iroquois lineages certainly had multiple functions during the pre-contact and early contact periods. In addition to being the fundamental political segments of Iroquois society, lineages were residential and ceremonial groups. Part of the breakdown of the lineage structure was no doubt due to the inability of white administrators and military personnel to cope with an acephalous political system. They saw chiefs and made a series of assumptions about social inequality and the primacy of certain individuals over others. This factor alone would not have been sufficient to bring about a breakdown of the lineage system, however. But the disruption of lineage landholding and hence of residence pattern brought on by Reserve settlement and sedentary agricultural pursuits, and the disruption of lineage ceremonial functions brought on by Christianity, were probably sufficient severely to weaken the structure. The collapse of the economic and ceremonial functions of lineages was, in turn, responsible for their partial loss of political function.

A society cannot exist without a political system, but political systems can be largely destroyed or rendered ineffective. The view of the Canadian government must have been that the political system at Grand River had either been destroyed by social change or should be rendered ineffective. The government wanted to substitute a new bit of social structure based upon elective representation for an old 'undemocratic' feature based upon hereditary lineage representation. Their assumption that a hereditary government is 'undemocratic' is justified to an extent; the question of 'democracy' does not arise in acephalous societies with general economic equality. But during the Reservation period economic inequality gradually developed; a man farmed his own fields and did not share his produce with other members of his matrilineage or clan. Persons successful under the new economic system did not need to accept the assumptions of the traditional political system if it did not suit them – if they had no hereditary right to membership on the council. Thus, about 1924, the Six Nations people were confronted with a pair of alternative political structures: an elective council, made up of the prosperous minority, and the traditional hereditary council, disrupted as it was by the collapse of lineage functions. Whether because of the remaining functions of the old social structure, or because the hereditary council has never conceded the right of the elective council to decide on Reserve affairs, most people still give at least tacit support to the traditional system by refusing to vote. The recent acceptance of the electoral system by the Lower Cayuga Longhouse may represent the 'wave of the future'. It would be a mistake, however, to see contemporary factional politics as merely a phase in the transition from one political structure to another. These factions have existed, with minor changes, since 1924 and are based upon much older cleavages in Reserve society. Even if, in the next generation, the elective system is accepted by a majority, the character of the new political system will be strongly colored by the present factional system. The implication of this is that the contemporary system has been strongly affected by the previous acephalous system with its institutionalized moiety conflicts and absence of strong, consistent leadership roles.

NOTES

1. The material contained in this paper was presented originally in the South Asia Seminar of the School of Oriental and African Studies while the author was Research Fellow in the Department of Anthropology and Sociology there. I am grateful to the participants in the seminar, particularly Prof. C. von Fürer-Haimendorf, Dr F. G. Bailey, Dr Adrian C. Mayer, Dr P. H. Gulliver, and Mr Hugh Gray for penetrating criticism and stimulating discussion. Fieldwork in Govindapur village from October 1960, through April 1961, was made possible by a Ford Foundation Foreign Area Training Fellowship; work among the Grand River Iroquois from June through September 1958, was financed by a grant from the Lichtstern Fund of the Department of Anthropology at the University of Chicago. I have taken advantage of the discussion following the presentation of this paper at the Cambridge A.S.A. Conference to strengthen it at a few points.

2. Together with a number of others who have read Lewis's account of factions in Rampur, I think what he treats as factions might more profitably be regarded as Jat descent groups with clients and other appendages. Therefore, in identifying myself as a student of political organization like Lewis, I do not mean that I define faction as he does.

3. The idea of a 'neutral faction' does not fit well into the system I propose here, since I hold that factions appear only during conflict; otherwise, they may be regarded as something like 'latent social organization'.

4. In a discussion after the presentation of this paper Professor Firth argued convincingly that this definition of politics is too narrow, since it cannot easily take account of political events about which all participants are in agreement. I have – perhaps only temporarily – solved this dilemma by relegating events of this kind to the sphere of 'government'. In utilizing this definition, however, it is essential to regard what is ordinarily spoken of as 'competition' as a species of conflict, and, in general, to interpret conflict very widely.

5. All the names used in this section – including the name of the village – are pseudonyms. I have used a different name for each actor identified in this account, and have distinguished them by titles wherever possible. Thus, Siva and Hari are identified as 'Mukhya', the local term for a village headman; Krisnadas and Ramdas are called 'Mahanta', 'abbott of a temple'. I have added caste names for members of minority castes; persons not thus identified are members of the dominant Mahisya cultivating caste.

6. The term 'Progressive' is not usually employed on the Reserve to identify this faction. Looking for a convenient label to use in talking about them, I chose 'progress' because it figures so importantly in their rhetoric.

7. The distinction proposed by Siegel and Beals, under the definition I employ here, confuses some non-factional kinds of social conflict with factionalism, and misses what might be a very useful distinction between schismatic and pervasive factionalism. The term 'schismatic' might well be applied to situations, like that among the Ndembu, in which prolonged conflict leads to the fission of the local community; but if the division is between corporate groups, as in lineage fission, I would not apply the term 'factional' to the conflict.

Ralph W. Nicholas

REFERENCES

BAILEY, F. G. 1960. *Tribe, Caste, and Nation: a Study of Political Activity and Political Change in Highland Orissa.* Manchester: Manchester University Press.

—— 1963. Closed Social Stratification in India. *Archives of European Sociology* 4: 107-124.

BEALS, ALAN. 1959. Leadership in a Mysore Village. In Richard L. Park & Irene Tinker (eds.), *Leadership and Political Institutions in India.* Princeton: Princeton University Press. Pp. 427-437.

BENEDICT, BURTON. 1957. Factionalism in Mauritian Villages. *British Journal of Sociology* 8: 328-342.

CHADWICK, E. M. 1897. *People of the Longhouse.* Toronto: Church of England Publishing Company.

CURTIS, MICHAEL. 1962. Introduction. In M. Curtis (ed.), *The Nature of Politics.* New York: Avon Books. Pp. xxi-xxx.

EPSTEIN, T. SCARLETT. 1962. *Economic Development and Social Change in South India.* Manchester: Manchester University Press.

FENTON, W. N. 1955. Factionalism in American Indian Society. Vienna. *Actes* du IVe Congrès International des Sciences Anthropologiques, 1952. Vol. II: 330-340.

—— 1957. Factionalism at Taos Pueblo, New Mexico. Washington: Bureau of American Ethnology, Bulletin **164**: 297-344.

FIRTH, RAYMOND. 1957. Introduction to Factions in Indian and Overseas Indian Societies. *British Journal of Sociology* 8: 291-295.

GOLDENWEISER, A. A. 1915. Social Organization of the North American Indians. In *Anthropology in North America.* New York: G. E. Stechert & Co.

LASSWELL, HAROLD. 1931. Faction. *Encyclopaedia of the Social Sciences.* New York: The Macmillan Company. Vol. V: 49-51.

LEWIS, OSCAR. 1958. *Village Life in Northern India: Studies in a Delhi Village.* Urbana, Ill.: University of Illinois Press.

LINTON, RALPH. 1936. *The Study of Man.* New York: D. Appleton-Century Company.

MAYER, ADRIAN C. 1961. *Peasants in the Pacific: a Study of Fiji Indian Rural Society.* London: Routledge & Kegan Paul.

MORGAN, LEWIS HENRY. 1881. *Houses and House Life of the American Aborigines.* Washington: U.S. Geographical and Geological Survey.

60

—— 1901. *League of the Ho-de-no-Sau-nee or Iroquois.* Dodd Mead edition of 1901, reprinted 1954. New Haven: Human Relations Area Files, 2 vols.

—— 1928. *Government and Institutions of the Iroquois.* Ed. by Arthur C. Parker. Rochester: Researches and Transactions of the New York State Archaeological Society.

NADEL, S. F. 1951. *The Foundations of Social Anthropology.* Glencoe, Ill.: The Free Press.

NICHOLAS, RALPH W. 1963. Village Factions and Political Parties in Rural West Bengal. *Journal of Commonwealth Political Studies* 2: 17-32.

NICHOLAS, RALPH W. & MUKHOPADHYAY, TARASISH. 1965. Politics and Law in Two West Bengal Villages. *Bulletin of the Anthropological Survey of India* (forthcoming).

NOON, JOHN A. 1949. *Law and Government of the Grand River Iroquois.* New York: Viking Fund Publications in Anthropology, No. 12.

SCALAPINO, ROBERT A. & MASUMI, JUNNOSUKE. 1962. *Parties and Politics in Contemporary Japan.* Berkeley: University of California Press.

SCOTT, D. C., *et al.* 1911. Constitution of the Six Nations Iroquois Confederacy; Laws of Dekanawidah; Kane-kon-kets-kwa-se-rah (Condolence Ceremony). MS. on file in the Department of Anthropology, University of Chicago.

SIEGEL, BERNARD J. & BEALS, ALAN. 1960. Pervasive Factionalism. *American Anthropologist* 62: 394-417

TURNBULL, COLIN. 1961. *The Forest People.* London: Chatto & Windus.

TURNER, V. W. 1957. *Schism and Continuity in an African Society: a Study of Ndembu Village Life.* Manchester: Manchester University Press.

WALLACE, A. F. C. 1952. The Modal Personality Structure of the Tuscarora Indians as revealed by the Rorschach Test. Washington: Bureau of American Ethnology, Bulletin No. 150.

Peter C. Lloyd

The Political Structure of African Kingdoms

An Exploratory Model

It is now nearly twenty-five years since Fortes and Evans-Pritchard (1940) gave us our first classification of African political systems – into hunting bands, segmentary lineage societies and centralized states. Other social anthropologists have subsequently offered improvements on these categories; yet few have attempted to define the basic differences between kingdoms as varied, for instance, as those of the Yoruba, Benin, and the Hausa-Fulani emirates, to cite but some Nigerian examples.

Historians still tend to seek a common origin for, and consequent similarity in, African kingdoms. Thus Fage and Oliver (1962, pp. 44, 49) postulate the spread of a Sudanic civilization across Africa: 'The central feature of this civilization was the incorporation of the various African peoples concerned into states whose institutions were so similar that they must have derived from a common source.' Later they add 'that the formation of states . . . was a process which involved the deployment of a considerable fund of common political ideas'.

One common feature of African kingdoms is their complexity and this has undoubtedly contributed to the failure to differentiate between them. As we know them, most kingdoms have evolved during several centuries of existence. In most cases the divine or sacred king is hedged about with archaic rituals; a multitude of office-holders surround his throne, some wielding political power, others having merely ceremonial duties. In the colonial territory and the modern independent state it is often the rituals and ceremonies which have survived, while the traditional decision-making processes have been irrevocably changed. Yet to the historian a knowledge of those processes is vital. The political scientist studying the modern state is also interested in them, for the values associated with the traditional political system may either support or conflict with those of the independent state.

It is my contention that a useful contribution to the study of African kingdoms lies in the examination of the composition of their political elite – the group of titled officials who, by tradition, advise the king. I have accordingly selected three methods of recruitment to the political elite and constructed a model to illustrate some aspects of the political process associated with these three methods.

The plan of this paper is as follows: first, I shall outline the existing classifications of African kingdoms proposed by social anthropologists. Second, I cite a few of the difficulties that arise from the complexity of the kingdoms. Next, I describe the functions of government, discussing the nature of the policy-making process and introducing the concept of political conflict and the competition between interest groups. In the fourth section, I define the basic criterion for the model – that of recruitment to the political elite – and describe four other variables that I believe to be of importance to the political process. Later, I outline three specific types of political system illustrated in my model showing the principal types of conflict which occur and the possible changes that these will produce in these systems. But those are not the only factors producing changes in the political system and, in the fifth section, I consider the effect of demographic factors in a polygynous society, of conquest and foreign trade and of the decline in strength of corporate descent groups. Finally, I assess the applicability of this model in present-day research.

EXISTING CLASSIFICATIONS

In his own recent classification of African political systems, Murdock (1959) offers us 'African despotism' as Negro Africa's parallel to Wittfogel's (1957) 'oriental despotism'. He lists eighteen characteristics which he believes are to be found in most kingdoms. These may be summarized as follows: the ruler is a divine king, clad in distinctive regalia and living almost in isolation from his large court of queen mother or sister, royal wives, and palace slaves. His apparent absolutism is demonstrated by the abject prostration with which his subjects appear before him and his claim to own all the land and people of his kingdom. A corps of titled officials hold advisory and administrative posts, the two roles often overlapping. Succession to the throne is rarely by primogeniture and, during an interregnum, rival princes, each backed with his own band of followers, vie for the support of the electoral group of officials. The royal capital is a sizeable town, though perhaps moved with each new reign.[1] Permanently sited towns seem to develop, in my own opinion, only with a high degree of craft specialization and the growth of long-distance trade. These features will be familiar to Africanists. Marginal to the category of kingdom are those societies where the rulers seems to exercise ritual authority only (though this may be used to enforce political decisions) and those where rulers exercise undoubted secular power but lack most of the attributes of the divine kingship.

A more recent attempt to classify African kingdoms is that of Vansina (1962). By his definition, a kingdom is a sovereign political group, headed by a single leader who delegates authority to representatives in charge of the territorial units into which the country is divided. He too outlines the characteristics of the divine king and the administration of the kingdom. Taking as his starting-point the king who controls both the internal and external affairs of the provinces, he bases his classification on the degree to which the royal authority is delegated to the provincial rulers; this is an index of centralization, as he uses the word. I shall myself discuss the concept of centralization later in this paper.

In criticism of Evans-Pritchard and Fortes, it was soon pointed out that in not all the 'stateless' societies is the segmentary lineage the basis of political organization – in many of them age-grades or associations of titled men are dominant; nor is the lineage an unimportant social group in the 'states'. Yet the division into states and stateless societies has been upheld by successive writers and the concepts of segmentation, lineage, centralization, and the state have dominated attempts at classification. As set out, these concepts form dichotomized pairs – segmentation v. centralization, lineage v. the state.

E 65

Fortes (1953) has described the lineage as being incompatible with the state; where both exist there will be instability; the greater the degree of centralization the weaker will be the corporate strength of the descent groups.

Fallers (1956, pp. 12f, 277f) takes up and elaborates this point, showing that lineage norms (loyalty to lineage members) are incompatible with state norms and that chiefs and rulers who are expected to conform to both sets will be in a situation of conflict. This cannot be denied, yet the situation exists in all societies; the problems of Antigone are still not resolved although the state usually respects the husband-wife relationship. Again, an elected representative to any body has a double and often conflicting loyalty – to his own electorate and to the whole organization on whose governing council he sits.

Second, segmentation has come to be identified with any kind of pyramidal structure. As used to describe the social structure of the Tiv, for instance, it denotes the balancing of opposed units in the lineage structure at each genealogical level. Barnes (1954) uses the term in this way, asserting that the Ngoni have a lineage structure which continually segments on the classical manner of the Nuer or Tallensi, albeit within the structure of the state; the leaders of the various segments are the political elite. He criticizes the use of the term segmentary to describe the hierarchy of fixed and inter-nesting administrative units into which the state is divided. However, Southall (1956), writing of the Alur, uses the term segmentary state to describe a situation where the territorial sovereignty of the centre is recognized, though it may shade off to ritual hegemony over the margins of the state, and where centralized government exists, though peripheral centres are but weakly controlled, perhaps exercising legitimate force and possibly seceding from one state to join another.

The centralized state, according to Nadel (1942, p. 49), has territorial sovereignty, specialized office-holders, and a mono-poly of legitimate force. The degree of centralization often seems to be measured by the size of this specialist body of office-holders. Thus Mair (1962) defines as the essential characteristic of the state the appointment by the ruler of territorial agents of his own choice for the execution of his orders. She rejects as another 'kind of polity' the state in which authority below the king is in the hands of lineage heads. Evans-Pritchard (1948) says that the Shilluk king reigns but does not govern, that his importance is mainly ritual, and that it is wrong to use the terms state, government, or administration of the Shilluk kingdom. (Yet in the nearby kingdom of Kofa the kings, according to Huntingford (1955), definitely do hold secular power.) It seems as if the term centralized state could not, if we follow Mair and Evans-Pritchard, be applied to a constitutional monarchy. Kaberry (1957) has differentiated between the centralized state, where the king and his councils assume most of the tasks associated with government, and a federation, where the central government has a monopoly of power in limited fields only, or where the rulers of local units exercise nearly as much power as the centre. In similar vein, Lewis (1959) suggests differentiating kingdoms on the basis of their degree of centralization.

One of the most comprehensive of recent attempts at classification is that of Eisenstadt (1959). He retains the basic distinction between states and stateless societies, classifying the latter according to the politically important form of structures – segmentary lineages, age-groups, associations, village councils. His centralized chiefdoms (exemplified by the southern Bantu kingdoms, the Bemba, and the Ashanti, but explicitly excluding the Ankole, the Shilluk, and the Anuak) are divided into three categories: those where descent groups are important units of political action, those where universalistic groups of age-grades exist, and those with title associations (the last-named being exemplified by Dahomey and the Mende kingdoms). The first two categories are subsequently described as federated monarchies and centralized monarchies respectively; a few of the characteristics of each are described, some being, in my own view, falsely antithetical.

In a rather different vein there has been discussion of the applicability of the term feudal to these African kingdoms by Maquet (1961, 1962), Murdock (1959), and Beattie (1960). Much of the argument naturally revolves around one's concept of feudalism either as a very general term or as denoting a particular set of institutions found in medieval Western Europe. Those who use the term do so on the basis of the patron-client relationship which exists in many kingdoms; those who reject its use, Chilver (1960) for instance, do so on the grounds that the independent power of the European feudal lord against his king and the strength of his political, economic, and judicial domination over his subject peasantry are not characteristic of African kingdoms.

Standing apart from this main current of thought about segmentation and centralization, lineage and state, is the criticism of it by Smith (1956). He asserts that in any political system policies are made through a process of competition between segments of the society and that decisions are carried out through a hierarchy of administrative roles. Thus all political systems have their segmentary and hierarchical aspects and these concepts cannot be exclusively used for stateless societies and states respectively. But perhaps the most trenchant criticism comes from Easton (1959), a political scientist who took time from his studies of modern societies to examine the progress made by social anthropologists. He castigates the failure of the anthropologists to develop any broad theoretical orientation to politics, ascribing this to their preoccupation with general problems of social control, conflict, and integration and their reluctance to define the respective limits of political and other – social, religious, economic – systems. Easton offers a classification of African political systems which is based upon the differentiation in political roles; Smith does not propose any classification.

It falls outside the scope of this paper to elaborate in any great detail my own definition of the concepts of political and the political systems. My debt to both Smith and Easton will, however, be apparent in the later sections.

THE COMPLEXITY OF AFRICAN KINGDOMS

The cultural similarities between African kingdoms, such as those cited above by Murdock (1959) and also by Irstam (1944), still lead historians to think in terms of a common origin in the Nile valley or Near East for the institution of divine kingship. Thus Fage and Oliver (1962) postulate the spread westwards and southwards of a 'Sudanic civilization'. Whatever the origins of kingship, one can see in the past millennium the extension and expansion of kingdoms to form recognizable clusters – (i) the Western Sudan, Ghana, and Dahomey(?), (ii) the Nigerian cluster, (iii) the Congo cluster – the Lunda empire, (iv) the Southern Bantu cluster, the modern kingdoms being perhaps successors to the empire of Monomapata, (v) the Interlacustrine Bantu kingdoms of East Africa associated with the myths of the Cwezi and Bito and (vi) the kingdoms of the Eastern Sudan. Within each of these clusters there are, for obvious reasons, many similar cultural traits; yet the political structure of neighbouring kingdoms may be markedly different. Wilson (1939) and Read (1956) have described such differences for the Nyakusa and Ngoni respectively, and similar comparisons could certainly be made for the Yoruba kingdoms (Lloyd, 1954) and, I suspect, for many others. The very complexity of the structure of African kingdoms, together with the wide variations of structure within cultural areas, has tended to give an apparent uniqueness to each kingdom (fostered by the anthropologist anxious that his own monograph should be distinctive) which has deterred scholars from making comparative studies or attempting classifications.

Our study of African kingdoms is not made easier by their long and complex histories or by the difficulties in defining the teritorial limits of the power of their rulers.

Understanding of African kingdoms would be much greater if we knew more of their foundation and growth. But in most cases this is an almost closed book to us. In a few instances, and Buganda is a good example here, significant changes in the pre-colonial era can be traced (Southwold, 1961). Nevertheless, the analysis of myths and legends by the ethno-historian may in the future provide more information in other areas. Smith's (1960) reconstruction of the development of the political system in Zaria has demonstrated vividly how new rulers – here the Fulani and a century later the British colonial administration – retained so much of the pre-existing structure, keeping the titles though altering their roles.

The spread of kingship and of kingdoms is usually ascribed to a process of conquest; a powerful kingdom subdues its less powerful neighbour or extends its rule over hitherto chiefless peoples. This has undoubtedly happened on numerous occasions, yet it is not the whole picture. The Alur provide us with an example of the domination of one kingless people by another, resulting in the formation of little chiefdoms (Southall's segmentary state). Fulani mallams and pastoralists overthrew the Hausa kingdoms in the early nineteenth century (Smith, 1960). Certain Tiv travelled to the Jukun capital to receive regalia from the king, returning home as 'drum chiefs' to exercise power over their people (Bohannan, 1953: 35-7). Urhobo and Ijo leaders similarly received regalia from Benin. One cannot exclude the possibility that the traits of divine kingship may have been gained not by succession or by borrowing from neighbouring peoples, but by independent development from indigenous religious beliefs; it is difficult, for instance, to trace the origin of Nyakusa kingship.

With the export from Negro Africa of slaves and ivory and gold, a favoured position on a trade route (resulting in increased wealth and improved weapons with which to dominate one's neighbour) undoubtedly facilitated the growth of little kingdoms into vast empires.

In describing their kingdoms, anthropologists must perforce refer to the ethnographic present, or attempt to reconstruct the structure of the kingdom in the pre-colonial period, say at the end of the nineteenth century. But even if they must present us with a synchronic study, it still seems necessary that we should attempt to discover the age of the kingdom and its periods of growth and quiescence. For at these periods it must surely have undergone some structural change, new offices being created, old ones relinquishing political for ritual power. Yet any attempt to present a deterministic cycle of change based on economic criteria will fail in ignoring the calibre of individual rulers. One long-lived, astute monarch will perhaps strengthen the royal power over the subordinate chiefs; in other cases, and here again Buganda provides a good example, the infancy of the king may allow the chiefs to strengthen their own position against the monarchy (Southwold, 1961; Apter, 1961).

Another of our difficulties in examining African kingdoms lies in deciding upon their limits, for modern boundaries of colonial administrative units are frequently too precise. It is often possible to discern three levels of administration: the metropolitan area, the peripheral units, and the sphere of influence. The failure to distinguish between these has frequently bedevilled the discussion of the degree of centralization. The existence of peripheral units such as territories ruled or administered by royal princes has sometimes been held to constitute federation; yet it is not likely that Zaria emirate would be excluded from the category of centralized state, even though within its borders lie pagan tributary kingdoms. In many east, central, and south African kingdoms, the dominating group has, through shortness of time, failed to assimilate the indigenous peoples; thus one has the distinction between the true Lozi and the non-Lozi in the Barotse kingdoms (Gluckman, 1951). The relationship between the king and his chiefs in the metropolitan area is frequently different from that between the king and the rulers of the peripheral units of the kingdom. In discussing, and perhaps classifying, the political structures of African kingdoms, we must clearly state the unit to which we refer.

The majority of African kingdoms have been riven by secessionist tendencies. Units which have accepted domination in one century reassert their independence in the next, perhaps becoming powerful enough to overthrow the metropolitan ruler. Princes who fail to win the throne establish their rule over outlying areas of the kingdom, in uneasy relationship with the capital. It is perhaps a characteristic of most African kingdoms that the tasks carried out by government are not sufficiently elaborate and the administrative staff too weakly organized to ensure that the rule of the political leaders is felt equally within a few miles of the capital and on the margins of the kingdom.

Again, the distinction is not always clearly made between the political structure of the central government and that at the village level. Nadel (1942) has given us a clear description both of the central government of the Nupe emirate at Bida (clearly a highly centralized state, as this term would be used by himself and most others) and of village government where local policy is made and disputes are heard by a council of lineage heads. We have no difficulty in keeping these two structures in separate compartments; but we must remember that the individual villager lives subject to both forms of government; that two different sets of political norms are involved, and that the villager's attitude towards authority, for instance, cannot be related exclusively to one or other set of norms.

THE NATURE OF GOVERNMENT

Evans-Pritchard and Fortes complained that political philosophy offered very little help in the analysis of African societies. But the last twenty-five years have seen, particularly in the United States, the rapid development of political sociology as a distinct discipline. Drawing on the sociological concepts of the Weber-Parsons schools and reviving interest in some almost forgotten political scientists of the early years of the century, scholars are becoming more interested in the nature of government (e.g. Easton, 1953; Almond, 1960). Their methods are of direct relevance to the study of African kingdoms.

Anthropologists have indeed been interested in the functions of government, but the question that they apparently ask is, 'What does government do?' Thus Schapera (1956), Kaberry (1957), and others describe the functions of government as the preservation of the society from external attack, the maintenance of internal order, the organization of complex activities affecting the welfare of society, the validation and maintenance of the structure of authority in the society. If one asks 'What is government?' the reply must be (following Easton) (i) the expression of interests or demands, (ii) the making of policy decisions, laws, or orders, (iii) the putting into effect or administration of these decisions, (iv) the adjudication of disputes that arise over the implementation of the decisions, and (v) the maintenance of public support for the governing body.

In their studies of African political systems, anthropologists have, in fact, described the administrative structure, but have tended to ignore the process of policy-making. Vansina's article (1962) is a vivid illustration of this point; he devotes much space to descriptions of tax-collecting and judicial processes, yet gives but a passing reference to the councils that usually advise the king. The reason for this failure to examine the policy-making processes stems partly from the nature of the fieldworker's situation.

So often where meetings of the councils of chiefs are informal, it is said that the king makes all the decisions; the fieldworker is not always living in the capital, and even if he is, he is not allowed to watch the interplay of ideas between the king and his advisers. Furthermore, while colonial native administration has preserved vestiges of the traditional administrative process that one can still watch in action, the traditional process of policy-making is often lost as rulers take their lead more from the administrative officer than from their titled chiefs. On the other hand the important rituals and ceremonies are still usually performed, in part at least, in public. These symbolize the traditional political norms and are vital to the study of the ideology which maintains the political structure. They have consequently received ample treatment by the anthropologists, though in the descriptions of these rituals it is often difficult to see how much is but an archaic survival with little relevance to the modern structure.

If we are to understand the government of African kingdoms, our emphasis must shift from the administrative structure and rituals to the process of policy- or decision-making.

Policy-making

Policy is made by a group of men – in the case of an African kingdom the king and a body of title-holders – whom we may call the political elite. But these men do not reach their decisions from the whims of their own thinking. Policy is determined by the competition between the interest groups in the society – that is, groups of people having shared interests who seek to influence policy. Thus we must ask first: how are these interests expressed or articulated, aggregated and finally transmitted to the political elite; second, how is the political elite recruited, and how far do they represent the interests in the society; third, how do the political elite communicate with the masses – the remainder of the society not of the political elite?[2]

In the near-subsistence agricultural economies of the African kingdoms, the prime economic interest is land and the rights to control, exercise, and alienate its use. Political interests include the right of the individual to represent his views to the governing councils of his community and the facility to protect all his interests and rights from infringement. The values of the individual, and in particular his religious beliefs, form another category of interests. Finally, the privileges which an individual holds constitute a further category.

People with similar interests may, and usually do endeavour to, form groups for the purpose of expressing these interests. These groups may consist of individuals who have nothing in common but a single shared interest; in African societies, however, it is more usual to find groups based on age, descent, or territorial residence in which a considerable number of interests are shared. In this context, the territorial group is often a village or quarter whose members are closely related by common descent or affinal relationships.

Shared interests however do not necessarily mean expressed interests; we must ask whether the members of the interest group meet formally or informally, and what are the frequency of and attendance at meetings, the status of members within the group and their role at the meetings, and the range of topics that the members feel to be proper at the meeting. We must ascertain the leadership of the group and its selection. Finally, we should establish the manner in which leaders of groups with similar interests or of diverse interests meet to discuss and aggregate their various points of view, ultimately expressing them to the political elite. (An emphasis on social structure has led many anthropologists to provide us with an elaborate analysis of the genealogical intricacies in the lineage, without telling us what the lineage members ever co-operate in doing, what are their corporate rights to land, to titled office.)

Who are the political elite? In modern societies, it is becoming recognized to an increasing degree that many decisions are made not by popularly elected representatives but by a host of unnamed persons of influence, sometimes designed as 'the Establishment'. Shall we be out of fashion in imagining that decisions in African kingdoms have been made by the titled office-holders and not by untitled men of influence? The risk does exist; yet it does seem that in most kingdoms men who have the ear of the king are in fact granted titles. Thus we may define the political elite as the holders of chieftaincy titles – or, if these are too numerous, of the more senior titles.

These men by virtue of their office, have a number of privileges not shared by the masses. They enjoy leisure and are often freed from any form of manual labour; their food and housing may not seem to a European to be greatly different from those of the masses, but within the limits of the local economy their diet is richer, their food supply assured, their houses larger, their clothing more extravagant. They enjoy a larger number of wives. The exercise of authority is pleasant to most men and is rewarded by deference from the masses.

Lasswell (1952) has described the recruitment of the political elite as the essential criterion of government; it will form the basis of our own model. Some titled offices may be rigidly ascribed statuses, being allocated according to a rule of descent, such as primogeniture, or of age – the oldest living member of the group holding the office. Other titles may be open to any member of the society, or they may be restricted to certain groups, as where a title is held by a lineage. What qualifications earn titled office? We may distinguish here between achievement within the political structure and outside it: in the former case a man gains a title or is promoted to a more senior office as a reward for loyal political service to or within the political elite; in the latter case political office is a reward for outstanding achievement outside the political sphere – in trading, for instance. Three factors may be important in determining a man's success in gaining office: First, the personal favour of the king or other members of the political elite – this favour being based on ties of friendship, descent, or affinal relationship or clientship. Second, wealth, which may have been acquired solely by the candidate himself or contributed by his kin. Third, a personal following of kin, age-mates, friends, or clients. Wealth indicates a man's ability or, if it is contributed, his personal following; it guarantees that he will be able to maintain the prestige of the office, especially if generosity is one of the norms of chieftaincy. A personal following indicates a capacity for leadership, a necessary attribute for an office-holder who has to ensure the acceptance of policy decisions by the masses. The weight given to these factors, in any kingdom, will demonstrate the degree to which the titled office-holder has achieved his position by virtue of his personal qualifications or as a representative of a group. (Those two qualities are not, of course, mutually

75

exclusive.) The foregoing discussion of factors affecting the achievement of office apply most pertinently to titles bestowed by the king and his senior chiefs. But they will also apply in part to offices filled by election within a descent group, in this case, however, the adherence to group norms (perhaps in opposition to those of the kingdom) will probably rank as the most important factor.

The political elite represent, to a greater or lesser degree, the interests of the mass of the people. But, holding extensive privileges, they themselves form an interest group for the protection of these privileges against the masses, who may resent supporting the elite. Furthermore, the members of the elite may have been recruited in a number of different ways – lineage heads, royal princes, senior slaves, and palace favourites; each of these sub-groups holds privileges perhaps slightly different in quality or quantity, and each is intensely jealous of encroachment by a rival sub-group.

At the head of the political elite stands the king, so often termed a despot. We may try to define the rights constitutionally held by the king; more realistically we may assess his power in terms of what he can do without suffering deposition or rebellion; this may be considerable in the case of those kings usually termed divine. But a despot is often defined as one who pursues his own interests, or as a ruler against whom there are no legal means of control[3]. These definitions give a false picture of the African ruler; rather should we use Bentley's (1908) formulation of the role of the despot as one who mediates between various interest groups in the society – those of the masses and those of the political elite. The king's decisions reflect his assessment of the importance of each group to the maintenance of the integrity of his kingdom, and thus indirectly to the security of his own office. Even where the king may be removed only by assassination and rebellion, there are many ways in which he may be coerced by his subordinate chiefs. They may refuse to perform certain rituals, thus endangering the kingdom; they may impose economic sanctions, as in refusing to transmit to the king his share of tribute; they may boycott the palace, thus overtly demonstrating the popular disapproval of the king. For his own part the king may employ against his chiefs those sanctions which are usually wielded by the powerful over their subjects – fine or imprisonment, deposition or suspension from office, deprivation of land, and banishment. But he usually has few physical means of enforcing these decisions save with the support of a majority of his chiefs. His most terrible sanction is perhaps his royal curse, the fear of supernatural retribution by the royal ancestors, or the withdrawal of that protection which derives from participation in the royal rituals.[4]

'The king makes all the decisions,' say so many African subjects; 'the king can do no wrong,' they continue. When disaster does hit the kingdom a scapegoat must be found. It may be alleged that the rituals of installation were not properly performed (as was the case with the late Awujale of Ijebu, a Yoruba kingdom) and that the king is not therefore infallible and endowed with supernatural power to rule well. Deposition is then regarded as a proper measure. In other cases, however, the scapegoat may be found among the king's subjects. In secular terms the charge may be made that he was ill-advised by his senior chiefs, or, if he is not thought to be bound by such advice, that the chiefs were working against him. In ritual terms, the disaster may be attributed to the failure of a priest to carry out the due rituals.

Administration

From the king to his nearest subject runs a chain of authority – orders are passed from one office-holder to another, each ranked in an heirarchical scale. But the men involved are most often the very members of the political elite who, in advising the king, are responsible for the policy decisions; the most senior advisers are also the most senior administrators. This double role has tended to obscure, in African socetes, the disitinction between the decision-making and administrative processes.

Here one might refer again to the variables used by Easton (1959) in his tentative classification: the distinction made between political and social roles in the society, the differentiation and specialization between political roles and the degree to which roles serve specific or multiple and diffuse functions.

In any society where the political elite are specialized office-holders they must be supported by tax or tribute levied on the primary producers. For unlike craftsmen, they cannot cost every service provided in terms of foodstuffs. Marxists tend to designate all tribute of this nature as exploitation (Potekhin, 1960), though when used in a perjorative sense this term might be restricted to cases where the tribute was squeezed from an unwilling subject population to maintain not only the political elite at an extravagant level, but also the whole group from which they are drawn – let us call it the ruling class – members of which do not carry out political duties. The administrative tasks in the African kingdom tend to be restricted to the collection of tribute, the organization of quite local projects (building a road, or the chief's house) and the mobilization of an army. In few African kingdoms are there signs that labour has ever been organized for public work on a large scale as in the hydraulic enterprises of the 'oriental despotism'; the ruins of Zimbabwe or the Ijebu *eredo* (Lloyd, 1959) are isolated examples belonging to a distant age.

The administrative units – tax units, labour gangs, regiments – over which these office-holders are placed are, once again, units of agnates or uterine kin, age-mates, territorial units, or units based upon some other criterion. The membership of these units is often similar to that of the interest groups described above.

Two features seem common throughout most African kingdoms. First, the tribute is not collected in its entirety into a central treasury from which the titled officials are paid salaries; each office-holder (and here arises the necessity for the members of the political elite to hold administrative posts) retains part of the tribute paid to him, either by the individual subject or the lower-ranking office-holder. Second, the tribute received by the king not only is used to maintain the palace establishment, and perhaps the relatives of the king, but also serves as an insurance fund from which the needy may draw. Hence derives the reputation of the African ruler for generosity – a generosity which serves to bind the allegiance of his subjects more closely to him.

The nature of political conflict
The unequal distribution of wealth, prestige, and power in a society leads to coercion and conflict. Those with the privileged

interests wish to maintain them; those without wish to share them. The main spheres of conflict are between the sub-groups of the privileged (the political elite in our discussions) and between the privileged and the masses. The political elite usually endeavours to unite whenever their interests are challenged by the masses.

Those without wealth and power have three courses open to them. They may seek to enter the political elite; they may seek to overthrow it, challenging the ideology on which it rests; they may weakly submit with little resistance. The first course will be resorted to where political office is open to all members of the society and a high degree of mobility into the elite is possible. In a society with a closed ruling class the second is the only active course for the masses. Social mobility and class conflict are the expressions of these two methods of achieving political power.

Policy decisions are determined through the interplay of the different interest groups, curbs on the actions of the members of each being provided by sanctions of the types discussed above. Those with privileges wish at least to maintain the *status quo*, a state of equilibrium, a state where power is balanced; if they have adequate control of physical force and if their ideology is accepted by most men, then the political structure may remain unchanged. But this lack of change is rare, for not only are there the abilities of the individual actors to consider but also such factors of change as we shall outline in a later section. A change in the political system may take one of three forms: the political elite will accede to the demands of an interest group, thus affecting the general direction of policy; the composition of the political elite will alter so as to reflect a new balance of power between the interest groups; the existing political structure will be overthrown and replaced by a new structure. Social mobility will result in the second of these possibilities; class conflict may result in the third if the ruling class refuses to admit the interests or the individuals of the striving groups.

The opposition of diverse interests results, in the long run, either in agreement, with the acquiescence of the weaker groups, or in the annihilation of the losing groups. In African kingdoms permanent opposition groups within the political elite are not found. A vote is never taken on any major issue, but all concerned voice their interests and the king, summing up, gives a decision which reflects the general consensus. Those who feel that another decision is possible or preferable may re-open the discussion at a later date. But if they can never accept the king's decision their only recourse is to overt rebellion or to departure from the kingdom with their followers. In societies with simple agricultural techniques and plenty of land, the latter course is easy. On the other hand, open societies are prone to stifle rebellion by recruiting the outspoken critics into the political elite so that their own interests become those of the latter group.

Anthropologists have in recent years tended to stress the integrating functions of conflict. But as the term conflict becomes more popular, its meanings become more diverse. Three broad usages may be distinguished.

An example of conflict often cited is the contest for a throne between rival candidates and their supporters. Here, each of the contestants is striving for identical ends and is probably using identical means. The articulation of the norms of kingship during the interregnum do indeed tend to reinforce these norms and to serve to unite the society. But I would prefer the term competition for such a conflict.

In earlier sections I have been using the term conflict in a very different sense. Here individuals or groups are not seeking identical ends but different ones; each has its own concept of an ideal society which differs from that of its rivals. Furthermore, each is prepared to use means of attaining these ends which its rivals may consider to be illegitimate. The Marxist concept of the class struggle is a conflict in this sense. In an African kingdom, an example is the contest between commoner chiefs and royal princes or palace servants for positions closest to the king.

Both conflict and competition produce social change – the former when one group succeeds in its aims, and the latter when one contesting group succeeds so often as to lead to the virtual extinction of the rival.

I would, furthermore, prefer the term role incompatibility for role conflict – in the sense, that is, of an actor being expected, by different actors, to perform roles which are not compatible with one another.

Centralization

Finally let us examine again the question of the degree of centralization of the African kingdoms. All kings are sovereign; they are supreme in their kingdoms; theoretically there is no limit to their legislative power, though they may be restrained by custom. An impressionistic estimate of the degree of centralization is often derived from the number of men hovering around the palace apparently engaged in administrative tasks, but this is an imprecise measure. Three criteria are more useful.

First, the sphere of competence of the government. As we have seen earlier, there are spheres which are held not to be the concern of government and its laws; family relationships are the principal examples and give rise to the supposed opposition between family and state. Where homicide is dealt with through the family or clan feud, or where a family head may put to death his son or wife for an offence without any legal actions being taken by the government, then these matters may be said to lie beyond the competence of the law. At the other extreme, where loyalty to the kingdom transcends even the closest family bonds, we often speak of a totalitarian government.

Second, we may examine the degree to which constituent units of the kingdom may act independently of the king. Thus if the constituent units (probably descent groups or territorial divisions) may make war on a neighbouring kingdom or on each other, the king being unable, unconcerned, or unwilling to support or repress the war, we could speak of a fairly high degree of decentralization. Again, if no right of appeal lay to the king in judicial matters, cases terminating at a lower level, we should again speak of decentralization. In African kingdoms, the adjudication of certain offences, homicide for instance, is not only bound to come before the courts but is frequently reserved to the king and his senior titleholders. One ought, I think, to assess the degree of centralization by this criterion, according to the powers which may be wielded by the king rather than to the number of occasions on which they are so exercised. Thus we would not designate a kingdom decentralized simply because *most* disputes were settled at a family or village level.

Third, the term centralization has been used to describe the degree of control exercised by the king over the office-holders in the administrative heirarchy. All the office-holders hold their posts, at least indirectly, from the king. Thus the Yoruba chief who is elected by his lineage is installed with great ceremony in the palace by his king; he swears to serve both his king and his lineage. Even where the king himself ostensibly chooses his closest advisers, his choice may be forced on him by external circumstances. In every kingdom we may, however, try to assess the effect of the king's personal choice in the highest appointments. A more valuable test is the right of the king to transfer an office-holder from one administrative unit to another or to demote him or depose him from office. Again, we may distinguish those administrative systems where the king directly appoints and controls every minor office-holder from those where each office-holder (subject perhaps to ratification by the king) appoints those ranking immediately below himself. Here again, however, we must remember that the actions of the king may represent not his own whims but the pressures of his senior chiefs or of interest groups.

I have used the term decentralized as the antonym of centralized. But as we have seen above, earlier writers have contrasted centralized and federated governments. I feel that the use of the latter term is unfortunate. In a federal system the constituent units have certain powers reserved to them by a constitution which is either written or implicit and which is binding on both the local and the central government. In many cases it may be claimed that the local units exercised the said powers before the establishment of the federation. A federation does not exist when the central government merely delegates by statute powers to local units – as the British parliament delegates to local government councils. Every government must delegate some powers to local administrative units if the machinery is to work smoothly. Although corporate lineages may be powerful interest groups and units of administration, it would be wrong to term the kingdom composed of such lineages 'a federation of lineages', even when the lineage might be said to antedate the kingdom, for the lineage may not claim legal equality with the government of the kingdom. True federations seem rare among African kingdoms, that of Ashanti (Rattray, 1929; Busia, 1951) being among the best-known examples.

A MODEL

By the complexity of their political systems. African kingdoms do not lend themselves to classification into a few neat categories. The selection of one or two criteria as the basis of the classification leaves too much to be ignored; examples are distorted to fit the prearranged categories and odd juxtapositions occur. Even if one plots societies along a single continuum, as Easton (1959) advocates, one is unable to use any but the simplest criteria.

A more profitable approach would appear to be in the construction of a model which might be used to illustrate the political processes at work in different types of kingdom. I am here using the term model in a mathematical sense – i.e. a set of variables so interrelated that changes in the value of any one of them will be associated with changes in the values of the others. It is a model which helps to explain political processes; it is not a model in the sense of an idealized or simplified description of the structure of any particular African kingdom in its totality. Once it has sufficiently illuminated political processes the model will have done its duty. The model is synthetically constructed; nevertheless, in building it I have continually held in mind the African ethnographic data.

Later I shall present three variants of the model. Some African kingdoms may seem to approximate closely to one or other of these variants and it may seem possible to classify kingdoms on the basis of such similarities. Yet many kingdoms will display features illustrated by two or all three of our variants; these must not be thought of as deviants from an ideal type.

Bases for the model

In discussing the nature of government, we stressed two themes: the composition of the interest groups and the membership of the political elite. As we have seen, earlier writers (such as Eisenstadt) tended to classify political systems according to the dominant grouping of the population: descent, age, or territorial groups. But a lineage, for instance, may be in interest group (holding corporate rights in land and a political office), an administrative unit, or a social group with little political importance, being concerned perhaps with the religious practices of its members or with inheritance among them. Again, interest groups and administrative units may in a given kingdom be recruited according to different criteria. A classification of kingdoms based upon purposes served by each group in the society would become very cumbersome.

Instead we take as our own starting-point the recruitment of the political elite – those titled chiefs (excluding the king himself) who make the policy decisions of government. An initial division is made between the kingdoms where these offices are open to almost all members of the society and those where they are reserved to persons of certain closed social groups. We may in fact scale the openness of any political system, but for the purposes of this paper it will be more convenient to select three positions which seem to be of common occurrence in Africa.

In the former kingdoms – the 'open' societies – we may distinguish two methods of recruitment. In one type we have fixed constituencies, each of which is represented by a member. In modern societies, these constituencies are usually territorial units. In African societies it is common for each descent group to be represented on the governing councils of one of its members. Titled office is thus open to all men inasmuch as each descent group holds a title whose incumbent is elected from among all male members of the group or is the oldest man of the group. We will base one variant of our model on the election of the title-holder by and from among the members of the descent group and term this variant representatative government.

In the second type of open society the titles are not held by and confined to specific groups but are ranked hierarchically within a political association; any man may start at the bottom of the ladder and move towards the top. The rungs of the ladder may be designated in a number of ways: (i) administratively – a man rises from village head to district head to divisional head, (ii) in terms of duties in the palace – one begins as a humble courtier rising to higher offices often expressed in terms of duties in the palace but nevertheless carrying administrative responsibilities, (iii) in a military organization. In each case the highest-ranking title-holders are the closest advisers to the king. Let us term this variant government by political association.

In the 'closed' societies, political office is reserved to members

84

of a ruling class which forms but a small proportion of the total population. This ruling class may be designated by ethnic differences, as between the Hausa and Fulani, or Tutsi and Hutu (Maquet, 1961); by a system of ranking of descent groups, the royal lineage being at the top, as among the Swazi (Kuper, 1947); or as an hereditary aristocracy, not organized into a few descent groups but possessing a culture distinct from that of the masses. In few of these societies, however, is the ruling class completely closed to upward mobility from the masses. It is quite possible that political offices within the ruling class are allocated in the manner of one or other of our open societies – the ruling class being, if considered in isolation, an open society. But a stratification of the type found in African kingdoms is frequently characterized by the progressively greater prestige of those closest by birth and marriage to the kingship – members of the royal lineage and especially those most closely related to the reigning king being the most highly ranked. We shall thus take, as our third variant a structure in which the most important titled offices are held by those men who are closely related to the king; we may term it government by royal aristocracy.

One might construct further variants, for instance one in which the political elite was drawn exclusively from palace slaves, probably born outside the kingdom. Such a structure, in which the free population has no political power, is difficult to envisage in practice and it does not seem worth while to continue its consideration.

We thus have the basis for three variants of our model. In many African kingdoms we do in fact find features of each variant represented – the king is advised both by lineage heads and by freeborn and slaves who have been promoted to high office. But the composition of the political elite in these cases is rarely static; certain sub-groups increase in power while others decline. By isolating them in our variants we may more easily study the conflicts which arise in given situations and determine the changes in the political system.

Other variables

In selecting these bases for the variants in the models, I have consciously taken three methods of political recruitment which seem to occur most frequently in African kingdoms. In amplifying the model, I have chosen four variables which ought, I feel, to be fully considered in the examination of the political system of any African kingdom. They are ones which have, only too often, been understressed in recent monographs.

The variables which I have selected are: (i) the political power of the royal lineage – an important question in view of the role of the king in the societies under discussion; (ii) the rights in land – the prime source of livelihood and therefore the dominant economic interest; (iii) the control of physical force – the army and police forces; and (iv) the preservation of individual rights.

It will be apparent that the variables selected concern the locus, not only of political power in its narrowest sense, but also of military and economic power. The fourth variable concerns the administrative potential of those wielding power. Thus one would expect to find a strong degree of inter-relationship between the variables.

First, I would expect to find associated with each of my basic types of recruitment a particular set of values for the other variables. It is these sets which I have presented in my later description of the three variants of the model. Data from Nigerian kingdoms, particularly those of the Yoruba, Hausa, and Benin, seem to support my hypothesis. Its application to other African kingdoms is hampered by the lack of data; many monographs fail to tell us, for instance, how the senior chiefs are recruited. One should not expect kingdoms to conform exactly to the variants of the model to be presented, for their political structures are usually far from static. Wide divergencies would, however, repay investigation.

Second, the values of any variable may change, either as a result of internal political processes – the competition and conflict which I describe as being appropriate in each of my variants – or of external factors of change, such as conquest, which I describe below. I would expect a change in one value to be followed by changes in the others. Thus: a new weapon is introduced, its control being confined to a particular group – the political power of this group is thus increased – they may seek greater control over land rights against the individual farmer; or: a council of commoner chiefs develops into an aristocracy – it will strive to increase its military and economic power. Such is the complexity of African kingdoms that the detailed sequence of possible changes is vast. Furthermore, our knowledge of the pre-twentieth-century history of these kingdoms is so meagre that we cannot with certainty describe changes in their political structures. It will be difficult to find data which will enable us to give greater precision to the assertion that the variables are interrelated to any high degree. Yet our model will be of use to the historian in his efforts to interpret his scanty facts.

1. *The royal lineage.* The installation ceremonies of the African king usually symbolize his withdrawal from active participation in the affairs of his own lineage; he assumes an office in which he reigns impartially over all his people. The man and his office remain distinct, and rebellion against a particular king is clearly different from revolution against the kingship. Nevertheless, the relationship between the king and his nearest relatives, in particular the members of his own lineage, may remain close. The status of the royal lineage is an important variable in the political systems of African kingdoms.

The power of the members of the royal lineage may be measured according to four criteria: (*a*) their rights to titled offices associated with policy-making – at one extreme they may be debarred from holding any such offices, though they may hold titles conveying largely administrative duties or responsibilities solely within the royal lineage; at the other extreme they may be among the most eligible candidates for the most senior chieftaincy titles; (*b*) the royal lineage may exert economic power through its control of large areas of land (or among pastoral peoples, through its ownership of cattle); conversely the royal lineage may have land which is sufficient only for its own members' agricultural needs; (*c*) members of the royal lineage may hold special privileges such as exemption from taxation and payment of tribute, death duties, and the like; they may receive gifts from the ruling king, thus participating in the wealth of the throne; conversely they may be liable for the same imposts as non-royals and receive no gifts from the king; (*d*) close kin of the king may be in a position to act as intermediaries between the king and his subjects, receiving gifts from the latter for their services; on the other hand, they may be barred from entry into the king's apartments in the palace and may have less contact with him than the non-royal chiefs.

Each of these four criteria may be scaled along a continuum from minimal to maximal rights, powers, or privileges; the sum of the four positions represents the political power of the royal lineage.

2. *The rights in land.* His rights to his land are the African farmer's prime economic interest. We may distinguish between those rights held by the farmers, either individually or corporately, and those held by the king, as head of government (Lloyd, 1962). The latter usually concern the control of land use and the right to certain rare products of the land or its fauna. In many African societies, where land is plentiful, usufructuary rights are not described with any high degree of precision; exact definition comes with land shortage and its commercialization.

However, it happens frequently that these usufructuary rights pass to the members of the political elite, so that it is they who ultimately hold rights of ownership while the farmers working on the land are their tenants. The legal status of the political elite may take several forms. Title-holders may be placed in administrative posts, perhaps controlling territorial units, in which they collect tribute and admit newcomers to the unit; usufructuary rights to land – its allocation and alienation – remain with the indigenous occupiers. But where the political elite is acquiring slaves who must be settled on land, or where the ruling class is expanding in number, the king may claim, and delegate to his officials, the rights to allocate all *vacant* land. Extending these rights, the king may claim that land becomes vacant on the death of the man cultivating it – i.e. usufructuary rights cease to be heritable and, although the farmer's son may in fact continue to work on the land, his succession must be approved by some overlord. This official may perhaps be entitled to evict any farmer who displeases him; and so the rights held by the farmer cease to be either permanent, alienable, or heritable. It is usually misleading to use English legal terms in describing African land rights, but a point is sometimes reached, as in Buganda with its *mailo* land, where, by a very slight twist of words, an administrative official becomes a land-owner in the English legal sense.

The use of valuable trees is, in West African societies at least, often taken to demonstrate ultimate rights to land; the administrative officials may exercise these rights over trees in order to buttress their claim to rights amounting to the ownership of the land against the farmers who, for centuries perhaps, have used it.

Our criterion in this variable concerns the allocation of rights in land between the mass of the people and the political elite. At one extreme, rights amounting to ownership are held by the individual farmer, or more usually are held corporately by members of village or descent groups. At the other extreme, these rights of ownership are held by members of the political elite, either by virtue of their office or because their wealth from land makes them most eligible for office; land-holding and political office may not correspond exactly, both being associated, however, with the ruling class. The farmer, at this extreme, is an insecure tenant having no permanent rights in his land and none to pass to his children or to alienate to other persons.

3. *The control of physical force.* An essential aspect of government lies in the ability of the political elite to use force to ensure obedience to its orders. A kingdom usually has an organized army and/or police force, but an important variable is the degree to which the political elite can manipulate this force to its own ends, to use it against internal rather than external foes. The important criteria are the control over offices or military leadership and the control over specialized weapons or highly trained military groups.

If the army (or police force) is composed of all adult men, armed with home-made weapons – bows and arrows, spears, clubs – it will be of little use to the king or his advisers in the event of total rebellion; they will not be able to enforce any unpopular measure on the whole population. Their weakness will be greatest if the army units are led by men selected by or from among the mass of the people; it will be less if the army is led by men closely linked with the political elite, being selected, perhaps, by them.

On the other hand, the army, or its main units, may consist of a specialized fighting force. Specialization may be by recruitment or by weapons. The king may have a royal bodyguard composed of slaves owing allegiance to him alone. The ruling class alone may provide the fighting element, the masses being used as carriers or cooks. In both cases the warriors may receive special training. Where horses or guns are available their supply, in the African kingdom, can usually be controlled by the political elite, who will allocate them only to their followers. The supervision of overseas trade is thus an important issue.

Furthermore if leadership posts in the army are hereditary, and there is little scope for the able warrior to reach a high office, the army will be of limited use in aggression. Conversely, a kingdom bent on external wars of conquest must organize an army led by the most talented.

Thus at one extreme we have an army composed of all adult men popularly led and furnished with such simple weapons as are possessed by all men. At the other extreme the effective corps in the army consists of a specialized body of men, drawn from the ruling class and having a monopoly of horses or guns.

4. *The preservation of individual rights.* In many African kingdoms there is little specialization of roles among the political elite and the same men both make the policy decisions and stand at the head of the administrative hierarchy that implements them.

Two themes interest us. First, the degree of control by the supreme authority, the king, over the administrative and judicial officials ranked below him. The orders of the king must be obeyed to the letter; the judicial process should not controvert the duly established laws. Smith (1960) has admirably illustrated the means used by the Fulani emir of Zaria to establish his control over the judicial structure of his kingdom. The variables in this theme have already been cited in our discussion of centralization.

The second theme is the protection of the individual from maladministration or injustice. Where the titled official administering a group is a member of that group – e.g. the elected chief of a lineage – the group will be able to apply numerous sanctions to control the behaviour of the official (his roles as an administrative official and as elected leader may well be incompatible). At the other extreme is the administrative official who is posted to a territory where he is virtually unknown and is liable for transfer within a few years. There are few sanctions that the individual who claims that an injustice has been done can employ against this type of official.

The man who feels, for instance, that he is being too heavily taxed has two avenues open to him. He may move to another district – an impossibility if he is bound to the land in serfdom and difficult if a move means sacrificing the rights to land of a lineage member for those of a stranger in his new abode. Second, he may appeal against the decision imposed on him by the administrative or judicial official. If his appeal can only be made to and transmitted by the very man whose actions are being questioned, it will not get very far. For the appeal to be successful, either there must be a recognized legally institutionalized means of taking one's complaints to a more high-ranking official in the hierarchy, and ultimately to the king himself; or one must have the assistance of an influential patron who will intercede on one's behalf with the higher official. If the patron's rank is considerably higher than that of the official against whose decision the appeal is lodged he may be able to coerce him into moderation.

In those societies where appeal through a legal hierarchy of courts is either not possible or not effective, a man may safeguard his rights through the system of clientage or patronage. These two terms have, however, been used indiscriminately to embrace a number of different phenomena; a rather detailed examination seems necessary here.

By clientship we denote a relationship between two persons who are not kin but stand in positions of superiority-inferiority to one another; the client is dependent upon his patron. The establishment of the relationship is marked with exchanges of gifts and possibly oaths of loyalty. In discussions of feudalism, however, the examination of symbolic creation of the relationship often seems to override that of the exact nature of the relationship itself. Several aspects of this relationship may be distinguished – social advancement, economic benefits, and administrative and judicial protection (Mair, 1961; Maquet, 1961).

In the open society, and particularly in the 'ladder' type where social mobility through the ranks of offices is rapid, one of the means of advancement is to seek the patronage of a person higher in hierarchy; he will press one's claims for promotion. Such a relationship may be transistory; it does not necessarily involve any grant of land by the patron to his client nor is it envisaged that the patron stands as protector to his client – all the usual channels of appeal are presumably open to the latter. Nevertheless, the client may go and farm in this patron's village, the patron may give some cattle to his client; but this is not the essential basis of the relationship, which is one of social advancement.

The classic types of clientship are associated with the closed societies, where the political elite is recruited exclusively, or almost so, from the ruling class. Here, we must distinguish between situations where the patron is also an administrative official set in authority over his client and those where he is not so placed.

As one example we may take the administrative official who is posted to a new area; his duty is to collect tribute, allocate land, settle disputes in that area; he maintains himself from a share of the tribute and service rendered to him. If he is liable to sudden transfer he will not bother to establish personal relationships with his people, but if he envisages permanency, these ties will probably develop. If the people are unable to move out of the jurisdiction of their new official or appeal against his decisions, they will probably seek to improve their lot by establishing personal relations with him – doing him favours or services beyond the minimum necessary. Thus a purely administrative relationship may develop at the instance of both parties into one usually associated with clientship.

In another example, let us presume that men can move freely from one district to another. An administrative official with vacant land in his district will seek to attract newcomers to swell his own tribute and personal following. To the loyal immigrant he will allocate land. For his part, the migrant will choose to live under an official who will uphold his interests.

These two examples must be distinguished from the third, where the client pledges his loyalty to a patron who is not the administrative official of his own district. The client performs personal services for his patron, the patron makes gifts to his client and may even give him cattle (a grant of land in these circumstances would be difficult to make without placing the recipient within the grantor's administrative jurisdiction; it is, however, possible in cases where the grantor's rights to alienate land are not derived from any political office that he may hold). The client expects his patron to uphold his interests when these are threatened by administrative or judicial action; he is his protector. It would perhaps be preferable if the term clientship (or its inverse – patronage) were restricted to those relationships typified in our third example.

Clientship (in its widest usage) may give to the client a degree of protection and some economic rights over land or cattle. To the patron, it yields an income from tribute and services and a personal following; both may be important to him in his own striving for higher political office. Only where the relationship cannot be severed by the client, or where the client cannot seek another protector, can the patron with impunity be harsh and vindictive to his clients.

Clientship is often fostered by members of the ruling class – and in particular of the royal lineage – who hold no office. They may trade their influence at the palace for the gifts and services of their clients. Members of royal lineage who are not eligible for political office may still use their personal influence in this way; and inasmuch as they win the following of a large number of clients their influence as a group is increased.

The client may forsake farming or his craft, and exchange his services for free board and lodging in his patron's house. The patron, if he is a titled administrative official, uses his clients as his auxiliaries. The term bureaucracy is sometimes used for structures in which this obtains and where the political offices themselves are distributed largely by the personal favour of the king. We do find here a limited degree of that specialization which is associated with bureaucracy, but most of its other traits are usually absent. The client does not have regular duties, the hierarchical relationship between clients is ill-defined, there is no

93

consistent system of rules defining the role of the client, the impersonality of bureaucratic relationships is absent, the advancement of the client depends on the personal favour of his patron before his actual ability. The clientship system is in fact the antithesis of bureaucracy as defined by Weber.

Ties of clientship cut across those of kinship. The rise of European feudalism is often ascribed to the failure of kindred or descent groups to provide sufficient security for their members. Nevertheless the relationship between the patron and his client is often idealized in terms of kinship, the patron acting as a good father or family head would towards his children.

This somewhat lengthy discussion of clientship has been occasioned by the rather muddled manner in which the topic has often been treated in anthropological literature. Let us return, however, to a final consideration of the means by which the rights of the individual may be safeguarded. At one extreme there exists a formal system of courts where the complaints of a man are justly heard; intermediate is a court system which is not effective since the defendant and the judge are the same person; at the other extreme, the individual has no redress in any court and must seek the protection of a person who is as powerful as the man against whom he complains. This variable may be further elaborated by considering the degree to which the court members or patrons are of the same interest group as the complainant. Thus our scale varies from a just court of law in which sit the elected representatives of the masses to a system of clientship in which the patrons are members of the ruling class, and the clients members of the masses.

FACTORS OF CHANGE

In my three variants of the model I shall stress the changes in the political system that may result from the conflict between different interest groups. Nevertheless I shall also indicate how changes in the balance of power between these groups might be affected by other factors. Briefly let us examine some of these other factors of change in a little more detail. The most important seem to be: (1) demographic changes resulting from polygyny and the uneven distribution of wives; (2) the aggrandizement of the political elite as a result of conquest or the control of external trade; and (3) the decline in importance of descent groups. The first of these factors must be considered in all kingdoms; the second will not be appropriate in all cases. The decline in the importance of descent groups is closely related to changes in the political system, though some of its causes may not be political by nature.

1. *Demography*

Most African societies are polygynous, for a large number of wives is usually a demonstration of wealth and prestige. The wealthier or more powerful section of the population will therefore increase in size at the expense of the weaker and poorer sections. Thus Zaria was conquered at the beginning of the nineteenth century by a small handful of mallams and pastoral Fulani; today 25 per cent of the population claims Fulani descent (Smith, 1960). If one century can radically change the numerical structure of the society, we must ask whether the political elite of the kingdoms have any conscious demographic policy.

Open societies are more likely to pursue an assimilationist policy – all persons eventually becoming members of the dominant ethnic group while the subordinate groups grow extinct. Where the society is composed of unilineal descent groups, those groups from which the political elite are drawn, or which have the higher-ranking titles, will tend to grow at the expense of the remainder. Specific methods for adoption into the lineage will hasten this process. The assimilation process is much faster where cognatic descent is traced and especially where not only do the men of the dominant group seek wives from outside the group, but the women are not discouraged from taking husbands from a less prestigious group. The Lozi provide a good example of an assimilationist people (Gluckman, 1951).

In a closed society, it is in the interests of the ruling class to remain a small group; yet polygyny produces rapid expansion. Two solutions are possible: the ruling class may restrict polygyny; the Tutsi of Ruanda seem to have accepted this policy, for after centuries of domination they still number only between 10 per cent and 20 per cent of the total population (Maquet, 1961). The other solution – that of the English aristocracy – is for the junior lines which fail to achieve titled offices to descend to the status of the commoner masses. This process too is facilitated where unilineal descent groups are weakly organized; it is hindered where other factors act to maintain the corporate strength of descent groups. The members of the junior lines may resist this apparent demotion and attempt to retain influence with the king and political elite through clientship systems.

The royal lineage constitutes a special problem, for its members are liable to bask in the reflected glory of the kingship even when they share few of its privileges. As the Shilluk say, there is always the danger that the royal lineage will swallow up the rest of the society (Evans-Pritchard, 1948). Three means of controlling its size are commonly found. First is the removal of members of the royal lineage by the killing of powerful princes, exiling them to distant provinces or expelling them from the kingdom. But the succession wars can take only a limited toll in numbers. Second, descendants of kings may either be ascribed to their mothers' lineages, as in Buganda (Fallers, 1960) or by a less formalized process be adopted into them (as among the Yoruba). Third, the status of lines in the royal lineage furthest from the kingship may descend to that of commoner lineages.

2. *Conquest and trade: the redistribution of wealth*

Conquest rewards the political elite with tribute, booty, and slaves. Even where those rewards are shared by the whole population, it is usually the king who receives the greater share. The acquisition of a large force of slaves by the king may enable him to establish an armed bodyguard and thus considerably strengthen himself against his chiefs. In times of conquest the increasing palace establishment is largely financed from the tribute collected; but in defeat or stagnation this establishment is not always quickly reduced. The palace looks to its own people for support; the masses are more heavily taxed, and may begin to resent the political structure, which brings them few benefits. Opposition may be met with repression – with terror and greater cruelty of punishment.

The conquered territories pose an administrative problem for the ruling political elite. The Yoruba solution is to make lineage chiefs the overlords of conquered towns, but this presupposes a well-developed administrative structure in those towns and a relatively slight degree of control and taxation (Lloyd, 1960). The granting of conquered areas as fiefs to loyal supporters of the king, making these men into administrative officials, is likely to cause some reorganization in the basic political structure.

With conquest there is initially a net flow of people as slaves from the conquered territories to the metropolitan areas. Where the slave owners are mostly members of the political elite they must have control over the allocation of vacant land so that they may settle these new dependents. This right over land may not have been previously held by them.

The wealth of African kingdoms was considerably increased as they were drawn into European trade, exchanging slaves, ivory, or palm oil for imported manufactured luxuries (Davidson, 1959). In many of the kingdoms of the Guinea coast, Bonin, Warri or Dahomey, the control of this trade was in the hands of the king; he received a levy on all goods exchanged and licensed certain men, usually those holding political office, to trade with the Europeans. Thus wealth remained coterminous with political power. At the other extreme are societies where the ruling class considers it beneath its own dignity to trade, and this occupation is therefore reserved for the commoners. Intermediate is a position where the organization of trade is quite separate from the political system but wealth gained in this way forms one of the main avenues to titled political office; the Yoruba are a good example in this case. Trading can result in greater accumulation of wealth than farming or craft industry, and may lead to the creation of a bourgeoisie which rivals the established ruling class, seeking political power for itself.

In African kingdoms, however, private traders have not developed into a bourgeoisie. Several factors may be considered to account for this. The profits of trade may be used in conspicious consumption or in investment; the main possibilities here being in land and slaves. But acquisition of these may be difficult for the trader, though they remain the prime means whereby a ruling class retains its privileged position. Trading businesses are the creation of an individual genius and difficult to transmit to heirs who are only too likely to divide and exhaust the fortune in a few years; inheritance by all male children makes it unlikely that one will be allowed to continue the father's business. Perhaps one of the most important factors is the belief of the trader that his wealth is due to his own ability and good fortune and that his children should follow their own predetermined fate; the idea that he might buy them a status equivalent to his own is alien to his philosophy. Lastly, the political elite may control the accumulation of wealth by imposing high taxes and death dues on the wealthy man and by victimizing him if his influence becomes too great. Alternatively, they may bestow titled political office on him so that his main interests become those of the political elite and no longer those of the merchant body.

The control of wealth may enable the king and the political elite to acquire and monopolize the supply of new weapons – horses and guns; they may build a specialized fighting force separate from the army of the masses; they may indulge in wars of conquest.

3. *The decline of descent groups*

Our distinction between the variants of an open society – the representative and the political association types – is correlated with the importance of corporate descent groups in the former and their weakness or absence in the latter. We may suggest a few factors which constitute to the decline in importance of these groups.

First, they may lose their corporate rights. The title held by the group may decline in political importance, retaining ritual functions only; it will cease to be a prize to be sought by members of the group and they will seek other avenues of political expression. This change in the status of the office may well be the result of a weakening of the power of the descent group for reasons outlined below; yet it will hasten the decline of group solidarity even further. Usufructuary land rights which are being exercised are perhaps unlikely to be seized from the descent group, but it may lose the control of vacant land to the political elite, so that the members of the group have to seek fresh allocation from this elite rather than from their own descent group.

Second, the descent group may lose its corporate character through the dispersion of its members. Freedom to move presupposes a sufficiently low density of population – i.e. the existence of vacant land to move into. But the movement may have several causes: soil exhaustion; accusations of witchcraft; desire to evade the authority of a father, headman, or chief; an expanding population through natural increase or through the capture of slaves. An inheritance pattern in which the house or farm passes to one son only, obliging others to seek new houses elsewhere, is an important factor; such a system is encouraged where farms are not easily divisible into economic units – the Buganda homestead, for instance, with the banana grove next to the single house of the farmer. Dispersion means that descent group members can no longer meet together frequently; they have fewer interests in common. The group cannot conveniently be used as a unit of administration.

Third, the solidarity of ties between members of a descent group is weakened by ties of clientship in which loyalty to one's patron may rival or be incompatible with that toward one's kin. The descent group is also weakened when hereditary wealth produces a new social stratification in the society.

THREE VARIANTS

In this section, I present three variants of the model based upon the three selected types of recruitment to political office. In each I shall describe the values of the other variables that seem most appropriate. The political process, expressed in terms of conflict and competition between groups, will be shown to differ in each of the three variants. Very briefly, I shall indicate some of the political changes which these processes, or other factors, seem likely to produce. One could, of course, postulate a much greater variety of situations.

1. *Open: representative government*

By our earlier definition, the political elite, the titled chiefs, in this variants are selected by and from among the members of the descent groups which compose the society. Each descent group is of the same status; its most senior chief is of equal status with others of the same grade, although a formal ranking is unavoidable. The kingship is held by the royal lineage – a group which in many kingdoms traces its descent from the supposed founder of the town. The king and chiefs rule the society. It is sometimes said of kingdoms of this type that the society is really a federation of descent groups, that the descent groups are virtually independent units and that the king is merely a ritual figure-head uniting them. But this is not necessarily so. The Yoruba chiefs are not lineage heads but the selected representatives of their lineage on the governing council of their town (Lloyd, 1960, 1962). Although much daily activity *is* organized within the lineage, the king and chiefs are responsible for a large number of public tasks usually associated with government – they alone may declare war on neighbouring kingdoms, they organize the clearing of roads and of new markets (work groups being recruited on the basis of age or lineage), they sit as the highest judical court, having original jurisdiction in cases of homicide and treason. As Gough (1961, p. 506) writes of the matrilineal Ashanti: 'it is perhaps in such states that the lineage achieves its height of collective legal responsibility and its strongest structure of authority'.

Let us consider the dimensions of our four variables which seem most appropriate to this variant of the model. The royal lineage has very little power, its members are not eligible for the higher chieftaincy titles, they do not control land, they have no privileged access to the king, and they are liable for tax in the manner of non-royals. It is the descent groups which corporately hold the land on which their members farm and live. Thus these groups are not only land-owning bodies (able to allocate and alienate their rights) but also residential units; they frequently have their own peculiar deities. They are, in fact, very strongly corporate groups, numbering perhaps several hundreds of people. Each titled chief is not only a member of the policy-making council but also the administrative head of his lineage. Lineage members who are dissatisfied with his role performance may upbraid him in lineage meetings and apply sanctions operative within the lineage. In this variant, leadership of the mass army often rests with a chief whose office is elective within a descent group; there is no fighting force with specialized weapons or training.

Meetings of the council of chiefs are regular and well attended; no lineage risks being unrepresented. Decisions are made by the chiefs, who transmit them to the king; he ordains them, his royal 'ban' imposing the most severe sanctions on disobedience. Political conflict operates within two spheres: between the descent groups and between the chiefs and their king.

Between the descent groups there exists competition and rivalry – for land, for chieftaincy titles, and for other privileges. The king, described as in most kingdoms as the symbol of his realm, is here a mediator between these groups with identical interests. His impartiality rests largely on the weakness of the royal lineage. The king unites the lineages, each of which has specific rituals to perform at his installation or burial. He is conceived of as a father-figure – his role is described in terms of family relationships.

The king has no physical force at his command by which he can quell disobedience to his orders; he must rely on the support of the majority of his chiefs and their people. But his sacred power is very great; his curse is feared; as a consecrated ruler he is believed to be incapable of misrule. A strong-willed king can therefore try to force his own ideas on his chiefs. He can divide them in their resistance to him by promising new titles to his supporters. But the chiefs may unite against their king; the sanctions at their disposal range from a boycott of the palace, through a failure to perform due rituals, to a demand that the king should leave the throne (perhaps by death). Such a balance between the king and his chiefs is upset if the palace establishment grows to the extent that the slaves form a royal bodyguard – a well-controlled little fighting force.

The incompatibility between lineage and state is said to produce instability (Fortes, 1953), but we need to see what instability means in this case. From our model (and from the examples of Yoruba kingdoms known to me), it would seem that the political system outlined might, if external events such as conquest or new economic opportunities are excluded, continue unchanged over very long periods. There would, perhaps, within each political unit, be a change in the size and influence of the descent groups. Where the kingdom is composed of a number of such units, each internally independent and owing allegiance to the metropolitan ruler, and where this dominance of the metropolitan town rests largely on its greater size, then secession by the more remote units is highly likely. In this sense alone can we term the kingdom unstable.

2. *Open: government by political association*

In our second variant, recruitment to the political elite is by appointment by the king; all members of the society (save only slaves, outcastes, etc.) are eligible; they are promoted through a hierarchy of ranked offices. The kingship is hereditary within the royal lineage. As in our first variant, the chiefs have both policy-making and administrative roles.

The dimensions of our four variables as here postulated are slightly different. The power of the royal lineage may remain weak. Land may be held not by descent groups but by the people inhabiting a village or quarter – people who do not form a single descent group, though they may be closely interrelated with one another by ties of descent and affinial kinship. The head of such a territorial unit allocates land to members of his unit, but the corporate rights of the group are more difficult to define, especially in relation to the rights of the king. Although the army is composed of all adult men with no specialized corps or weapons, it is possible to reward military ability with those political offices which have as their main role the leadership of the army.

Lacking rights in chieftaincy titles and land, the descent groups in such a society are corporately weak. They are often left with ritual duties only. The small village is the dominant unit. A man will express his interests variously through his village meeting to the village head and those above him in the administrative hierarchy, through his age-group, and perhaps through the title association to which he belongs. Since promotion in the title association depends to a large extent on the favour of one's superiors, clientship is common here as a means to upward social mobility.

In this system, there is strong competition for promotion between the individual members of the political elite, each backed perhaps by a following recruited in a number of different ways – by kinship, by co-membership of a village, by clientship.

Where the king may freely appoint, promote, and depose, the rivalry becomes more intense; tale-bearing leads to rapid rises or falls in the hierarchy and a feeling of insecurity of office is strongly felt.

The most senior chief in the political hierarchy is selected by the king as his right-hand man, yet he is also conceived of as the popular leader against the autocracy of the king, curbing his excesses. Such is the position in Benin (Bradbury, 1957) and among the Lozi (Gluckman, 1951). Although the king cannot control an armed force against his chiefs, his right to appoint and depose his advisers does give him a high degree of autocracy. This is often emphasized by the lack of any formal and regular meeting of the senior chiefs in council; views are communicated between individual chiefs and the king consults whomsoever he wishes. It is perhaps in political systems of this type that one finds the institutionalized Queen Mother performing the role of adviser and moderator to her headstrong son.

The chiefs of the political elite may combine against their king, although their interpersonal rivalry often makes this difficult. The king may counter this move by appealing directly to his people, accusing the chiefs of trying to enrich themselves at popular expense. With the decline of the lineage, its rituals become less important; their place is taken by more elaborate national rites in which the king is the leading actor. The dominance of the king, in a sacred and ritual sense, is thus even greater than in our first variant of the model. Again, the king can negate opposition by creating new chiefs, perhaps even a new grade of chiefs. The political elite is thus fragmented into a number of sub-groups each with its own privileges and competing with one another for power. In playing one such sub-group against another, the king becomes even more apparently autocratic.

Should the political elite of any period become entrenched in power, at the expense of their king, they could develop into a ruling aristocracy. This has in fact happened in Buganda (Southwold, 1961; Apter, 1961), where a number of factors have operated to produce this result: monogamy, limiting the number of children; planned intermarriage among the elite and the free tracing of cognatic descent and affinal links; the creating of heritable landed property divorced from political office (the

103

mailo land); and the ability of the elite to ensure a similar status for their children through education (in the Western sense) or through clientship and palace office (in the traditional manner).

In societies of this type the political associations are likely to grow in times of successful wars or favourable trading conditions. With the onset of a recession, the members of the political elite attempt to retain their earlier wealth and power; this can be achieved only at the expense of the common man of the kingdom (no longer can the conquered territory or the alien trader be exploited) and a period of repressive government with cruel punishments may result. In nineteenth-century West Africa, the bloodthirsty regimes of Benin, Ijebu, and Dahomey (all of which approximate to this variant) were contrasted with the apparent mildness of rule in the Akan and other Yoruba kingdoms.

In broad terms, political systems of this type seems relatively stable; they would not seem to be on the verge of transformation into another type, such as that suggested by our first or third variants. Yet within the system there is frequently a high rate of mobility into and out of the political elite and considerable personal insecurity of status. There may, too, be a continual formation of new title associations within the political elite as the king endeavours to counter the opposition of one sub-group by appointing more loyal supporters to new offices.

3. *Closed: government by royal aristocracy*

It must be stressed again that within a closed society recruitment to the political elite may follow the pattern of either of two previous variants. In this variant, however, we wish to study the political system where the highest political offices are held by close relatives of the king, usually members of the royal lineage. This is in marked distinction from our two earlier variants in which the members of the royal lineage were excluded from much of the political process and particularly from its policy-making aspects.

In the present variant, the members of the royal lineage not only achieve high political office but they also share in the wealth of the kingship; they may be absolved from taxation. Their close relationship with the king gives them opportunities to act as intermediaries. A well-developed system of clientship usually exists, on the one hand between members of the ruling class as a means of social and political advancement, and on the other hand between aristocrats and commoners as a means of protection for the latter and political following for the former. Members of the ruling class form a specialized fighting force; the commoners (such as the Hutu of Rwanda) merely act as auxiliaries.

In this system there is perpetual rivalry between the members of the royal lineage for high office. During an interregnum (and earlier too, in anticipation of it) eligible members of each lineage segment which may produce candidates for the throne contest among themselves; then the segments unite behind their chosen men and compete with each other. The newly installed king rewards his backers with high office, but these men are also his closest rivals. A vivid example of this type of competition is provided by Smith (1960) for the emirate of Zaria. The members of the political elite may be ranked according to the supposed seniority of their titles, but their influence with the king depends largely on the closeness of their relationship to him and the size of their personal following of kin and clients. The king meets his chiefs as he wills and not in a regular council.

This political system would seem to be, in its pure form, most unstable. It would be a rare kingdom in which the political elite was drawn exclusively from the royal lineage. Faced by the perpetual rivalry from other members of the royal lineage, the king tries to buttress his own power by granting political office to those who depend on him alone for this favour and not on their membership of the royal lineage – to affinal and maternal relatives, to loyal supporters from other groups within the ruling class, to slaves and lowly commoners. If he succeeds in recruiting such men to the political elite he may rule quite autocratically by playing one sub-group against another. He may even become strong enough to destroy his princely rivals completely by killing or exiling them. At this stage the political system, within the ruling class, probably approximates more closely to our second variant. But while the king is advised by senior members of his own segment of the royal lineage the latter will tend to curb any excesses or misrule on his part, for on the success of his reign depends, to some extent, their own chance of succession.

The dominated commoner class does not participate directly in the government of the kingdom; its members have no control over appointment of members of the political elite, though they may influence the selection inasmuch as they support, as clients, one or other candidate for office. The commoners may be organized on the basis of descent groups still holding substantial land rights; the ruling class will, however, seek to gain control of vacant land. It is in the interest of the ruling class that strong corporate groups and loyalties should not exist within the commoner class; bonds of clientship cut across class boundaries and link the king with his subjects. In the two previous variants, a common political ideology was shared by the political elite and the masses. In this variant the ideology of the ruling class, emphasizing its right to rule, may be rejected by the commoners, though the political elite will endeavour, through its control of rituals and the educational process, to ensure its acceptance. It happens sometimes that the king recruits a few title-holders from the more lowly commoners, thus giving the impression that an avenue of social mobility into the ruling class does exist.[5] Beattie (1960) relates that the Bunyoro king is seen as the 'ruler' of his people – not their father; this image probably extends to most societies following this variant. The features described in this paragraph will apply of course to the dominated class in any closed system and not simply to one in which the political elite is recruited from a royal aristocracy.

THE APPLICATION OF THE MODELS

I have presented three variants of a model, based upon the methods of recruitment to the political elite and amplified by the discussion of other variables; I have indicated the main spheres of political conflict in each. The model could, of course, be elaborated even further by incorporating other criteria which have been mentioned in this paper. It seems preferable, however, to keep the model as simple as possible and to apply it and the criteria raised to the examination of African kingdoms. I regard this paper more as a plea for the study of the political processes of African kingdoms on the lines discussed above than as a definitive description of the working of the model.

The model was designed to illustrate processes of change within a political stysem and it is tempting to see the variants, in the order in which I have presented them, as a historical sequence. There is a tendency to associate a strongly developed lineage organization with a more 'primitive' form of government, while the higher degree of specialization in political offices in many of the kingdoms like our third variant is taken to indicate a more 'advanced' type. For Polynesia, Goldman (1955) has presented three types of political system not unlike my own variants and has claimed that unilinear historical sequence can be demonstrated in this area. But there seems to be no evidence that African kingdoms change from a system represented in the first variant through that of the second, to that of the third. The political system represented in the third variant – the closed: royal aristocracy – is often the result of conquest and is therefore the first stage in a cycle of change. Again, the myths of the Yoruba indicate that most of their kingdoms were founded by conquest or some process of domination; their present political system, represented by the first variant, is the result of a long period of evolution. Some of the patterns of change have been indicated above, but it will be a long time before we are able to present any general scheme of political change in African kingdoms.

The model outlined here enables us to compare kingdoms in different cultural areas – the Swazi, Baganda, and Ashanti for instance; simple criteria help us to cut through the peculiar terminology and nomenclature that develop in each region; so that the scholar who feels familiar with one part of Africa feels lost in another. But a much more exciting task that awaits us is the comparison of neighbouring kingdoms in the same cultural area – the various Akan kingdoms, the kingdoms of the Interlacustrine Bantu or the Southern Bantu. Here, the cultural similarities, produced by centuries of conquest, migration, and other interaction, have often obscured the differences in the political system of each kingdom. The criteria which I have discussed in this paper will help us to make these comparisons.[6]

The usefulness of this model does not cease with the comparisons of African kingdoms in the 'ethnographic present' or their known recent past. It would be worthwhile too to examine whether the problems associated with the application of colonial native administration to each variant showed any uniformity. Was it always easier, for instance, to impose colonial rule on these societies already governed by a small closed aristocracy? Did all kingdoms of our first type share similar experience, in whatever part of Africa they were sited?

In the discussion of 'negritude' and 'African personality' it is sometimes suggested that there exists an African form or concept of government which differs from that of the Western and industrialized world. Yet the differences between the three variants of our model (which relate only to kingdoms) suggest that there is a wider range in traditional African political systems than exists today among the industrialized nations in spite of the oft-proclaimed communist-democratic dichotomy. One may still ask, however, if the alleged departure of so many new African nations from the patterns of Western democracy towards a one-party system can be explained in terms of the indigenous political systems.

The increasing use of the recent concepts of political sociology to analyse the traditional political systems of African kingdoms enables us to overcome the awkward traditional-modern dichotomy that has persisted for so long (Apter, 1955; 1961). In a crude way our first variant can be equated with the parliamentary system of representative government, our second with those systems where the single party dominates the political process. It could be argued that African peoples who have lived for centuries with a political system corresponding to our first variant, will find that a Western-style parliamentary democracy preserves many of their concepts of government; that those accustomed by a title association will accommodate themselves more easily to a single-party system. Nevertheless, the rapid rise of new ruling groups today can be compared with the much slower processes of past centuries which also made radicial changes in the political system. The Akan kingdoms were similar to our first variant, the present-day government of Ghana is more like our second; our task is to develop criteria and models which will illuminate these changes, seeing them not as peculiarities of the mid-twentieth century, but as examples of processes that have long been known in Africa.

NOTES

1. In a more recent essay, Murdock (1962) classifies the kingdoms of Nigeria into large and small states.

2. In some respects the analysis of pre-industrial societies is easier than that of industrial societies, for in the former men have fewer interests and perform fewer different types of role (Southall, 1959); groups based on age or descent predominate.

3. The latter seems to be the basis of the descriptions of Murdock (1959) and Vansina (1962).

4. Beattie (1959) has outlined the wide range of sanctions which serve to prevent the abuse of power in African kingdom.

5. Anthropologists who study this type of kingdom, Smith (1960) and Maquet (1961) for instance, seem to rely on informants from and to favour the ruling class, giving rather too facile an explanation of the integration of the kingdom and understanding the feelings of the commoners.

6. I myself hope to publish a comparative study of Yoruba kingdoms; they are so varied that one could, I believe, write a textbook on African government taking most of one's examples from this single people.

REFERENCES

ALMOND, G. A. 1960. A Functional Approach to Comparative Politics. In *The Politics of Developing Areas*, pages 3-64. Princeton: Princeton University Press.

APTER, D. E. 1955. *Gold Coast in Transition*. Princeton: Princeton University Press.

—— 1961. *The Political Kingdom in Uganda*. Princeton: Princeton University Press.

BARNES, J. A. 1954. *Politics in a Changing Society*. London: Oxford University Press.

BEATTIE, J. H. M. 1959. Checks on the Abuse of Power in Some African States. *Sociologus* 2: 97-115.

—— 1960. *Bunyoro, an African Kingdom*. New York: Holt, Rinehart & Winston.

BENTLEY, A. F. 1908. *Process of Government*. Evanston, Ill.: Principia Press.

BOHANNAN, L. & P. 1953. *The Tiv of Central Nigeria*. London: International African Institute; Ethnographic Survey of Africa, Western Africa, Part 8.

BRADBURY, R. E. 1957. *The Benin Kingdom and the Edo-speaking Peoples of Southwestern Nigeria.* London: International African Institute; Ethnographic Survey of Africa, Western Africa, Part 13.

BUSIA, K. A. 1951. *The Position of the Chief in the Modern Political System of Ashanti.* London: Oxford University Press.

CHILVER, E. M. 1960. 'Feudalism' in the Interlacustrine Kingdoms. In A. I. Richards (ed.), *East African Chiefs*, pages 378-393. London: Faber & Faber.

DAVIDSON, B. 1959. *Old Africa Rediscovered.* London: Gollancz.

EASTON, D. 1953. *The Political System.* New York: Knopf.

— 1959. Political Anthropology. In B. J. Siegel (ed.), *Biennial Review of Anthropology 1959.* Stanford: Stanford University Press.

EISENSTADT, S. N. 1959. Primitive Political Systems: A Preliminary Comparative Analysis. *American Anthropologist* 61: 200-220.

EVANS-PRITCHARD, E. E. 1948. *The Divine Kingship of the Shilluk.* Cambridge: Cambridge University Press.

FALLERS, L. A. 1956. *Bantu Bureaucracy.* Cambridge: Heffer.

— 1959. Despotism, Status Culture and Social Mobility in an African Kingdom. *Comparative Studies in Society and History* 2: 11-32.

FALLERS, M. C. 1960. *The Eastern Lacustrine Bantu.* London: International African Institute; Ethnographic Survey of Africa, East Central Africa, Part 11.

FORTES, M. 1953. The Structure of Unilineal Descent Groups. *American Anthropologist* 55: 17-41.

FORTES, M. & EVANS-PRITCHARD, E. E. (eds.). 1940. *African Political Systems.* London: Oxford University Press.

GLUCKMAN, M. 1951. The Lozi of Barotseland in North-western Rhodesia. In E. Colson & M. Gluckman (eds.), *Seven Tribes of British Central Africa.* London: Oxford University Press.

GOLDMAN, I. 1955. Status Rivalry and Cultural Evolution in Polynesia. *American Anthropologist* 57: 680-697.

HUNTINGFORD, G. W. B. 1955. *The Galla of Ethiopia.* London: International African Institute; Ethnographic Survey of Africa, North-Eastern Africa, Part 3.

IRSTAM, T. V. H. 1944. *The King of Ganda.* Stockholm: Statens etnografiska museum, New Series, Number 8.

KABERRY, P. 1957. Primitive States. *British Journal of Sociology* 8: 224-234.

KUPER, H. 1947. *An African Aristocracy.* London: Oxford University Press.

LASSWELL, H. D. 1952. *Power and Society.* London: Routledge & Kegan Paul.

LEWIS, I. M. 1959. The Classification of African Political Systems. *Rhodes-Livingstone Journal* 25: 59-69.

LLOYD, P. C. 1954. The Traditional Political System of the Yoruba. *Southwestern Journal of Anthropology* 10: 366-384.

—— 1959. Sungbo's Eredo. *Odu* (Ibadan) 7: 15-22.

—— 1960. Sacred Kingship among the Yoruba. *Africa* 30: 221-237.

—— 1962. *Yoruba Land Law.* London: Oxford University Press.

MAIR, L. P. 1961. Clientship in East Africa. *Cahiers d'études africaines* 6: 315-325.

—— 1962. *Primitive Government.* Harmondsworth: Penguin Books.

MAQUET, J. J. 1961. *The Premise of Inequality in Ruanda.* London: Oxford University Press.

—— 1962. A Research Definition of African Feudality. *Journal of African History* 3: 307-310.

MURDOCK, G. P. 1959. *Africa; its Peoples and their Culture History.* New York: McGraw-Hill.

—— 1962. The Traditional Socio-political Systems of Nigeria. In R. C. Tilman & T. Cole (eds.), *The Nigerian Political Scene.* Durham, N.C.: Duke University Press.

NADEL, S. F. 1942. *A Black Byzantium.* London: Oxford University Press.

OLIVER, R. & FAGE, J. D. 1962. *A Short History of Africa.* Harmondsworth: Penguin Books.

POTEKHIN, I. I. 1960. *On Feudalism of the Ashanti.* Moscow: Oriental Literature Publishing House. Paper presented to the 25th International Congress of Orientalists.

RATTRAY, R. S. 1929. *Ashanti Law and Constitution.* London: Oxford University Press.

READ, M. 1956. *Ngoni of Nyasaland.* London: Oxford University Press.

SCHAPERA, I. 1956. *Government and Politics in Tribal Societies.* London: Watts.

SCHNEIDER, D. M. & GOUGH, K. 1961. *Matrilineal Kinship.* Berkeley and Los Angeles: University of Calfornia Press.

SMITH, M. G. 1956. On Segmentary Lineage Systems. *Journal of the Royal Anthropological Institute* 86: 39-80.

—— 1960. *Government in Zazzau, 1800-1950.* London: Oxford University Press.

SOUTHALL, A. W. 1956. *Alur Society.* Cambridge: Heffer.

—— 1959. An Operational Theory of Role. *Human Relations* 12: 17-34.

SOUTHWOLD, M. 1961. *Bureaucracy and Chiefship in Buganda.* Kampala: East African Institute of Social Research, East African Studies, No. 14.

VANSINA, J. 1962. A Comparison of African Kingdoms. *Africa* **32**: 324-335.

WITTFOGEL, K. A. 1957. *Oriental Despotism.* New Haven: Yale University Press.

Aidan Southall

A Critique of the Typology of States and Political Systems

I. TYPOLOGY AND GENERALIZATION

Typology-makers are only anthropological butterfly-collectors (Leach 1961a, p. 3), we are told, and I agree with the general argument, though it is perhaps a little unkind at some points and is sufficiently important to merit further exploration. Continued effort in typology and classification may well be unproductive, except by way of arranging available material as a basis for a more advanced phase of structural-functional analysis which is both comparative and diachronic.

Typology is little more than a teaching aid, facilitating summary exposition, unless it gets us further on the road to valid generalization (cf. Kluckhohn, 1960; Murdock, 1960a).

Dr Leach's simple answer as to how satisfying generalizations can be made – 'by thinking of the organizational ideas that are present in any society as constituting a mathematical pattern' – is ambiguous in certain respects. To a large extent – and to establish just how far is one of the most important tasks of research – these organizational ideas are not the consciously stated norms or overtly expressed values of a society, but very often those latent functions of the system of which Merton has said that 'it is precisely at the point where the research attention of sociologists has shifted from the plane of manifest to the plane of latent functions that they have made their *distinctive* and major contribution' (Merton, 1957, p. 66). Examples of this are legion. Merton himself cites Hopi rain ceremonies, the Hawthorne Western Electric Studies, and Veblen's conspicuous consumption. Surely Leach's own major contributions, in uncovering the implications of matrilateral cross-cousin marriage and of the Trobriand category *tabu*, or in redefining Indian caste, have all been notable examples of this.

H   113

Lévi-Strauss labours the same point a good deal. He credits Boas with introducing the distinction between conscious and unconscious models. He insists that 'conscious models, which are usually known as "norms", are by definition very poor ones, since they are not intended to explain the phenomena but to perpetuate them'. Only finally does he grudgingly admit that 'many "primitive" cultures have built models of their marriage regulations which are much more to the point than models built by professional anthropologists' and such 'home-made' models might prove to be accurate, or at least provide some insight, and even if they are biased or erroneous this in itself is of significance (Lévi-Strauss, 1953, pp. 526-527).

If, then, when Leach refers to 'ideas that are present in any society', he means ideas that are unconsciously present, this surely should be made plain. This is more than a quibble because, once recognized, it brings into the open the fact that these organizational ideas are inferred not simply from the ideas expressed in a society but from the analysis of social action. It would be odd in the extreme to find that we had come full circle and once more only had to collect kinship terms (the labels of cultural ideas) without bothering about kinship behaviour, inquiring about religious beliefs, and ignoring ritual activity. The truth is that the organizational ideas can be arrived at and used only after the most exhaustive study, analysis, and understanding of the system of social action which constitutes a society. This is certainly borne out by the trend of recent anthropological studies of religion (Evans-Pritchard, 1956; Middleton, 1960; Lienhardt, 1961).

The Kachin concepts of *mayu* and *dama* (Leach 1954, pp. 73 ff; 1961a, pp. 81 ff) could stimulate a brilliant hypothesis in a fertile brain, but a model could be constructed only after exhaustive study of an extensive literature supplemented by intensive field-work. On this basis, it was possible for convincing clues to be suggested for the working of the model of Lovedu society, but in the absence of adequate field data the model remains unsatisfactory, incomplete, and unproved.

The organizational ideas are only a shorthand for the most significant patterns of social action and are arrived at only as the distant end-result of the painstaking study of social action.

Leach could not have improved upon Malinowski's analysis were he not himself a fieldworker and Malinowski's field data so good. The idea of Kachin cross-cousin marriage is at first essentially misleading, because the consistent group relationships to which the idea refers have very little to do with cross-cousin marriage, which is just a homely and symbolic way of describing them. Latent function is no doubt enshrined in the vernacular term, but the organizational idea is dispersed in the social activity of the Kachins and is not seen as such. The link between such organizational ideas and action is indirect and complex. It is not so much that approved action must conform to the ideas, as that individual acts or particular situations must be so interpreted that the various interpretations conform to the central organizational ideas, which is in fact often a tautology, since the latter may be nothing more than a deduction from the former. It is only when appropriate vernacular terms or usages happen to exist that the ideas appear thus to be implicit in the linguistic structure and in this sense enshrined in the people's culture.

In a lineage system, a large segment does not necessarily have to treat a small segment on terms of equality because their ancestors were brothers: rather, the small segment has to seek alliance and claim fraternal ancestry with another small segment, or even accept subordinate structural status within the large segment, by reinterpreting the relationship as filial instead of fraternal, so that not activity itself but the interpretation of it can be brought into conformity with the central organizational ideas. The Sinhalese *pavula* is the same kind of idea, 'a kind of Chinese box concept'. 'Since all members of the *variga* are relatives, any two of them can always represent themselves as being of the same "ideal" *pavula* by making an appropriate choice of common ancestor' (Leach, 1961b, p. 112). In other words, the organizational ideas do not directly control action, but only the interpretation of action. The primary interpretations of action, with continual adjustment of the basis for them, are the tenuous threads which link and reconcile action and ideas. This is more especially true of traditional societies. The causal influence of ideas in social systems is vastly increased when there are specialized roles devoted to their development and techniques for recording and disseminating them, none of which has been the case in most societies which social anthropologists have studied.

This whole argument may be flogging a horse that never lived, but it would seem unfortunate to condone the misunderstanding that social anthropology is moving in any simple sense from the study of action to the study of ideas. Hence the virtue of Leach's further suggestion of adopting algebraic symbols, which may more readily be accepted as standing for 'relationships and sets of relationships' (Leach, 1961a, p. 8) and are less likely to be taken as representing ideas without their action context.

Assessment of the utility of typologies or unidimensional classifications of political systems is inevitably part of the wider problem of rethinking the structural-functional model in social anthropology. Classification 'has very serious limitations' (op. cit., p. 3) but can be a useful stage in the process of analysis if understood in proper terms and not seen as an end in itself. It may be unfair to say that Radcliffe-Brown's instructions to compare societies with reference to one aspect (economic, political, kinship), is no more than classifying butterflies by colour, size, and wing shape. It may be no more, but should be taken to imply analysis from all these points of view, necessarily taking into account the very large number of factors into which these blanket categories would have to be subdivided, and above all seeing the factors *in their interrelationships* from *every point of view adopted*. Indeed, this is implicit not only in any functional analysis in the mathematical sense, but also in any construction of models.

You must carry out a very large number of different analyses of the same data. But in any one such analysis you have to decide on your factors, at the same time remembering that any such decision is partly arbitrary and that the analysis will have to be repeated not only with either more inclusive or more exclusive categories, but of course, with categories defined on totally different principles. All these are inevitably 'prior category assumptions' (op. cit., p. 4). But the most ineluctable prior categories of all are those of language and we cannot think, speak, or write without them. The dangers of prior-category assumptions can only be minimized if we constantly change our sets of categories and constantly redefine them. Yet this has to be done within the limits of mutual intelligibility in the continuous discourse of our discipline! A further major difficulty is that, of all the separate analyses with different sets of category assumptions which ought to be carried out on any significant body of material, only a very few can ever be published, most frequently only one. The writer presumably chooses his favourite set of category assumptions as the framework of publication, or the one forced upon him by extraneous circumstances. In any case his preference has often changed by the time publication is achieved and all we can do is give him the benefit of the doubt for all the other analyses which he should have done before having to come down to one for publication.

Hence, also, the importance of recognizing that we deal in partial analysis of partial systems. Our analysis is partial because we can never establish a functional model with complete logical closure without losing touch with our facts. (The systems we study are partial for the same reason.)

Where, at what point, does a system of classification turn into a model? Classification and generalization are not processes different in kind unless the practitioner makes them so. Classification into types seems an almost unavoidable stage on the road to generalization. At least, Leach himself used Kariera, Trobriand, and Kachin *type* marriages, as 'a very convenient shorthand notation' (op. cit., p. 59), in the process of achieving 'the comparison of models rather than of "whole cultures"' (op. cit., p. 104), while rightly insisting that 'the comparison must always take into account the whole range of institutional dimensions with which the anthropologist normally has to deal and must start from a concrete reality – a local group of people – rather than from an abstract reality – such as the concept of lineage or the notion of kinship system' (ibid.).

This is admirable. But it seems to me that Dr Richards's article on 'Some Types of Family Structure among the Central Bantu' (Richards, 1950), which Leach takes as a prime example of the limitations of comparison, is not just a typological exercise but a very useful piece of groundwork, perhaps not pushed quite far enough and failing to reach the level of generalization partly through deficiencies in the ethnographic evidence.

117

Since it is futile to aim at a Linnaean classification or typology of states or political systems, such attempts must be judged misguided.

II. THE RANGE OF POLITICAL ACTION

Without wishing to be held up by mere terminological questions it is necessary to mention some of the radical differences of opinion which remain on the nature of the political.

Schapera has argued for a definition based on function and not on means, accusing Weber of the latter with reference to a phrase in which he is actually defining political association (1956, p. 94). The fact is that Schapera does not attempt a definition of the political, or of political action as such. He gives highly overlapping definitions of political organization and political community, without clarifying the distinction. He brushes aside the crucial problems which most other Africanists have faced in this field, namely the definition and meaning of the political where roles are unspecialized and fields of authority and political action fluctuate and overlap. The problem is easy to solve for South Africa, he says, and each political community has its own territory and an official head or chief. The answer must be that the South African material is a special case and provides a poor basis for a definition applicable elsewhere. The attempt to treat Nuer or Dinka society in terms of exclusive territories and chiefs can only lead to self-deception (Mair, 1962, pp. 17, 38, 47). The same would be true of the Hadza, the Masai, the Gusii, the Luo, and a host of other African peoples.[1]

The function and means distinction is a red herring. An adequate definition will certainly include both, as Weber's does. It is remarkable that Mair appears to contradict Schapera's statement about his own definition, by saying that his phrase covers the means also (Mair, 1962, pp. 20, 16). Schapera not only has to stretch the facts by a crude insistence that the Nuer, Tallensi, and Andamanese have chiefs (1956, p. 39), but his definition of political organization (op. cit., p. 218) is so broad that it would often include a great deal of the ritual sphere, which should surely be kept distinct.

A definition based on the concept of power may appear to be

concerned with means from the point of view of the individual, but the system of allocating and controlling the use of power is functional simply in the sense that human society is impossible without it. The same is true of the economic allocation of scarce resources.

Smith is concerned, in my view rightly, with political action as 'an aspect of action' (1956, p. 71) but lays special stress on the distinction between administrative action and action 'which seeks to influence decisions of policy by competition in power' (op. cit., p. 48). It is the latter which he calls political action. He includes both political and administrative action in government. In other words, Smith wishes us to use the word government where most writers have used the word political. It seems that this usage is unlikely to catch on and will therefore increase confusion. While accepting the basis of definition, I would prefer to retain the term political for the general aspect which includes both administrative action and that 'which seeks to influence policy by competition in power'. Failing a better word, the latter will have to be termed policy action. It must be taken to include strategic, tactical, and legislative action.

The determination of policy is always an important arena for competition in power, but it is not the only one. Empirically, a great deal of competition in power is not concerned with influencing policy but with achieving administrative roles. It is here concerned with the way persons move in the system, not the way they change it. The distinction between administrative and policy action is important, and indeed quite close to commonsense, but in many small-scale societies it is not manifest and therefore concerns the analyst, not the member of society. Smith criticizes 'the mistaken conceptualisation of political behaviour as a special type of behaviour' and the 'arbitrary division of social life into planes of group relations' (op. cit., p. 71), such as, presumably, the political, economic, kinship, and ritual or religious. The point is certainly well taken, and surely well recognized, that these are analytic aspects of social relationships. But it is equally important to recognize the significance of the fact that in some societies certain activities, institutions, and roles are overtly specialized and largely confined to one or other of these analytic aspects and in other societies they are not.

The definition of these analytic aspects (by no means wholly satisfactory as yet from the point of view of logical closure), is part of the anthropologist's model, which he orders in numerous variations, with more particular detail yet still at a high level of abstraction, and relates to the manifest and latent models presented by empirical societies. If there is to be meaningful communication, the analyst's own definitions must clearly have an invariant matrix, but their relation to the variable cultural definitions of the same matters in different societies is of paramount significance. The weakness of Smith's framework lies in the fact that he endeavours to deal with this mainly through the concepts of office and corporation sole, which is both too cumbersome and incomplete (op. cit., pp. 60-68). The matter can be dealt with more adequately in terms of the concept of role differentiation, which is applicable to all the analytic aspects of social action, including both the administrative and the policy varieties of the political aspect. I agree with Smith in rejecting the restriction of political relations to interrelations of major groups alone (op. cit., p. 58). The intrinsically political obviously cannot be defined in terms of the concepts of political organization or political community, which must flow from it. On the other hand, it is true that Radcliffe-Brown's definition (1940, p. xxiii) is too directly tied to the use or possibility of use of physical force.

Following Weber, I consider that political action, or the political aspect of social relationships, is that which is concerned with power, ultimately sanctioned by the use of physical force. But this sanction may be extremely remote and indirect, yet axiomatically present in any context of command. For power is the probability that an actor can carry out his will despite resistance. Imperative control is the probability that a command will be obeyed. Authority is the legitimate exercise of imperative control (Weber, 1947, pp. 139-140). It is clear that political action usually takes the form of the exercise of authority, including both the giving and the receiving and implementing of commands. It is only in transitional situations that other forms of power, outside the realm of legitimacy, are exercised with the aim of achieving legitimacy. Although analytically transitional, such situations are empirically numerous and important. Some

120

social systems present the observer with the appearance of chronic quasi-legitimacy or perpetual transition. Part but not all of this ambiguity can be clarified by precise definition of the different spheres of legitimacy attaching to the various roles in a social system.

When a social act, a role, or an institution, has the exercise of authority as its primary goal, it is inevitable that we should call it political, although there is always a greater or lesser element of inaccuracy involved in so far as it is not wholly or exclusively political.

In a further refinement, Easton (1953, pp. 123, 146) emphasizes the distinction between power in general and power in a political context, defining political science as the study of the authoritative allocation of values as it is influenced by the distribution and use of power. This is surely very close to Weber's concept of authority in other terms. The point I would stress is that our terms should serve to draw attention to rather than gloss over or exclude the secular process in human society whereby specialized political roles have become differentiated from the matrix of more generalized roles and institutions.

If the necessary minimal consensus on meaning can be achieved to permit communication, there are two further points which require to be made. The first concerns role differentiation. The second concerns power within the family.

By role differentiation I mean the number of distinct roles to which separate meaning is attached in any social system and the process whereby the number and definition of roles so differentiated alter (Southall, 1959, p. 20). This is largely a refinement and extension of Durkheim's concept of the division of labour. The wide spectrum of African political systems receives much illumination from it. At the lower end of the scale of role differentiation are those societies which have been variously described as stateless, acephalous, uncentralized, or lacking in government, or politically non-organized, but which I prefer to characterize as lacking in specialized political roles. They have few or no roles whose primary goal is the exercise of authority. Authority and political action there are, but they are exercised through multipurpose roles in which they cannot be said to form the primary element. At the other end of the scale (in societies of high role

121

differentiation), there are numerous roles which we are justified in calling specifically political because that is their primary goal, even if not in the strictest sense their exclusive one. Lineage leaders, spear chiefs, and leopard-skin chiefs; age-grade elders, counsellors, and spokesmen (Gulliver, 1963, pp. 101-109); clan heads, and prophets all belong at the lower end of the scale, for several aspects of social action other than the political are fused in all these roles. Ritual or sacred chiefs and divine kings are intermediate. Chief ministers, client chiefs, formally constituted army leaders, and secular headmen usually come nearer the top end of the scale for the primary orientation of their roles is clearly political.

Now that we have well learnt the distinction between lineage and kinship organization, between family and descent group, it seems necessary to look again at the family from the political point of view. This is obviously important in the light of the 'authoritative allocation of values' stressed by Easton (loc. cit.). Without prejudice to the much greater permanence of corporate descent groups on the one hand and to more transitory situational networks of personal kinship on the other, it would appear that, in societies of low role differentiation, the family is necessarily a corporate group in which power and political action are of the greatest importance. For Weber 'a social relationship which is either closed or limits the admission of outsiders by rules, will be called a "corporate group" so far as its order is enforced by the action of specific individuals whose regular function this is, of a chief or "head" and usually also an administrative staff. These functionaries will normally also have representative authority' (Weber, 1947, pp. 133-134). But 'whether or not a corporate group exists is entirely a matter of the presence of a person in authority, with or without an administrative staff'. 'Corporate action' is either the action of the administrative staff, which by virtue of its governing or representative authority is oriented to carrying out the terms of its order, or it is the action of the members as directed by the administrative staff.

Can it be doubted that the family in traditional or low role-differentiated society is corporate and acts corporately, in terms of Weber's criteria, let alone the looser ones of Radcliffe-Brown (1950, p. 41)? As a limiting case, the family satisfies all the attributes. The important possible exceptions are the attributes of permanence and role interchangeability. In many unilineal descent systems the descent groups are far more permanent, and to that extent more fully corporate, than the family. Indeed, perhaps the more permanent the descent group the less permanent the family. Where descent groups are not so strongly developed, the family often possesses more permanent features, such as perpetual succession, which make it more clearly corporate. Where continuity rests upon property rather than upon descent, as in the Iban *bilek* family (Freeman, 1958), it is again more permanent and corporate; that is, its leading roles persist independently of particular incumbents. Having recognized these important distinctions, it is necessary to accept the corporate and political aspects of the family.

Men do on the whole endeavour to maximize the authority disposable by their society, just as they endeavour to maximize its wealth. The inherent limitations imposed upon these processes in systems of traditional authority are similar. Generalizations can be oriented meaningfully to the problem of the extent to which traditional political systems achieved what Weber called imperative co-ordination. The balance between ritual and political techniques is a central theme.

The political power of the family, that is the degree of authority exercised in and by it, is important in all traditional societies. The fundamental process through which the authority disposable by a society is increased and imperative co-ordination achieved is through progressive role differentiation. The differentiation of specifically political roles is most important here, but the functional interlocking of the social system is evident in the fact that increased political role differentiation cannot occur without repercussions in the rest of the system. In particular, political role differentiation cannot proceed beyond a certain point without a complementary differentiation of economic roles. Neither political nor economic role differentiation can proceed beyond a certain point without an appropriate technology, which is itself facilitated by such role differentiation. Within certain limits of role differentiation and technology there is room for quite different orientations of interest in a society, as between aggression and conquest, the valuation of order and harmony, or aesthetic and ritual elaboration. But granted this degree of tolerance for different directions of interest, or cultural focus as Herskovits would have called it, beyond this the limitations imposed by the level of role differentiation are ineluctable.

Although the family is too small to have a genuine administrative staff, the father is frequently the head in Weber's sense and it is possible for his son to act as his administrative staff. This can be equally true of mother's brother and sister's son in matrilineal and matrilocal systems. We normally think of the political in terms of adults, whereas in the family it refers largely to authority over women and children as legal minors. Political action occurs in the family, although the family cannot have strictly political roles. It clearly has the ultimate sanction of force and this has the most profound implications for the maintenance of order in society. The use and control of force are a fundamental feature not only of family life, but also of many peer groups, whether street gangs in towns or herding groups in villages. In age organization this is formalized. An important part of political structure, and training for political leadership, is therefore to be found in family and peer group in some societies and, of course, with varying degrees of legitimacy.

Dr G. K. Park has remarked to me that, among the Kinga of southwestern Tanganyika, it may happen that children beat up their father by the time they are ten or eleven years old, thus terminating his effective political jurisdiction over them. Indeed, the woman may be physically stronger than the man, though Kinga ideology states the opposite. The man should be the boss of the family; therefore, if a wife kills her husband in a fight, it must be stated to have been an accident at the trial, or else men would be admitting inferiority and the contravention of ideology in practice would be openly exposed (Park, 1962).

Beyond a certain level of political role differentiation, and assuming its implications for the role structure of the society as a whole it is inevitable that authority should be progressively withdrawn from the family, that is, the political aspect of kinship roles is transferred to newly differentiated political roles. However, most of this process occurs at a level of role differentiation higher than that associated with primarily traditional society. Kinship roles are the fundamental matrix from which other roles emerge, and there is an inverse relationship in any society between the political aspect of kinship roles and the level of political role differentiation.

The differentiation of political roles is also eventually at the expense of ritual roles, or perhaps one should rather say that, when there is a splitting of roles in which major ritual and political aspects have hitherto been fused, the differentiation of new political roles proceeds further than that of specifically ritual roles. The further role differentiation proceeds, the more diverse and heterogeneous are the persons with whom the individual enters into role relationships, especially in the higher positions of status. Social persons become less and less alike or interchangeable, because the possible and necessary role combinations become legion. Instead of the extreme of everything being done with the same people, each activity is carried out more and more with different people, so that a person's life is not contained within a limited number of groups, but in ever more numerous distinct but overlapping networks of role relationships. Although the alternatives are finite and patterned, the choice before the individual is much wider and the element of rationality in selection is greater also. Greater change is possible and higher mobility necessary. No longer does the performance of multifarious activities with the same persons and groups reinforce and intensify relationships between them. Repetitive action becomes conventional almost by definition and conventional action, if not actually the cause, is the most favourable ground, for the emergence of ritual. Societies of low role differentiation possess the most favourable ground, whereas societies of high role differentiation necessarily depend more upon specialized roles for the maintenance or initiation of ritual. The organic[2] structure of society renders people ineluctably interdependent and ritual is less necessary to hold them together in solidarity. Specialized authority roles enable order and security to be achieved by larger groups over wider areas. The ritualization of social relationships in general is not only less necessary but less possible (Gluckman, 1962, pp. 2, 49-50).

The balance between ritual and political role differentiation is one of the most important interpretative factors associated with the range of traditional African political systems.

For purposes of exposition rather than explanation three relevant typological ranges can be marked off on the scale of political role differentiation. The first corresponds to what have been called stateless societies, the second to what I have previously called segmentary states, and the third to unitary states. The latter range was one which certain historical African states were just in process of attaining and is predominant in the contemporary world, whereas the middle range is most important for this paper because most traditional African states, and almost certainly many in other parts of the world, were of segmentary type.

In suggesting the term segmentary state in an earlier publication I was mainly concerned to point out that, despite constant reference to African states, hardly any of them conformed to the recognized criteria of a state (cf. Easton, 1953, p. 109). The wheel seems to have gone full circle, and Vansina (1962, p. 330) implies that the point was almost banal because nearly all African states were segmentary. I am glad if this is now recognized, but further clarification is certainly required.

The distinction between hierarchical and pyramidal seems useful (Southall, 1956, pp. 248-251). The term hierarchical should be used of a political system only when authority is allocated from the centre in a *de iure* and a *de facto* sense. Of course, there is always the consent of the governed, but it is quite clear when right of allocation from the centre is regarded as legitimate by the majority in the sense that the enforcement of this right is also legitimate. The term pyramidal would be more appropriate for articulated structures in which the exercise of central authority depends upon consensual delegation to it by the component units in each case, without any stable recognition of the right to enforce and maintain this by coercion. This situation obtains not only in acephalous segmentary lineage systems and a number of other types of stateless society but in segmentary states.

A state is not segmentary only because it is composed of segementary lineages: this is an interesting special case. It is segmentary in the sense of its pyramidal power structure. If this concept of pyramidal were accepted, such states could be termed pyramidal in distinction from hierarchically unitary states and to avoid confusion with the wider sense of segmentary in which Smith claims that 'political relations and segmentation are synonymous' (1956, p. 64).

Strictly speaking, we have to consider two polar types of delegation by the public, which characterize opposite ends of the range of political systems. They may be designated associational and complementary delegation.

Associational delegation is a formally defined process occurring within an articulated system of specialized bodies or associations under the overall umbrella of the state. On the other hand, complementary delegation arises from the complementary opposition of segments, whether they are lineage segments or any other pyramidally articulated units, whereby segmentary leaders, or impartial persons occupying roles constituted for this purpose, are virtually compelled by situational exigencies to act with a certain temporary but legitimate and truly delegated authority, however frail or transient.

Associational delegation in various forms characterizes the most specialized states of the modern world, whether the process of delegation is supposed to take the form of popular choice between alternative candidates, or whether it is rather a ritual affirmation of candidates in power. In either case, importance is attached to the consensual basis of power. In associational delegation, it is certain that the delegation will occur and be maintained and reaffirmed as long as the system itself is maintained, for without delegation – the conferring of authority upon role incumbents at the centre – the system itself would collapse. But it is not certain to whom the delegation will be, since it is essentially an achieved role. Apart from the actual occasions of formal delegation, when ritual expression is given to the ideology that power is conferred upon the leaders by the people, the power structure is distinctly hierarchical, with adequate imperative co-ordination. Extreme forms of hierarchical system with absolute authority, where hardly even lip-service is paid to the idea of delegation from below, were characterized by Weber as 'Sultanism'.

By contrast, complementary delegation is contingent upon at least partially ascribed roles, it is essentially situational, and imperative control from the top of the pyramid may not outlast

the situation itself. If delegation occurs, it may be certain to
whom it will occur, but whether or when it will occur is by no
means certain (Gulliver, 1963, p. 107). None the less, although
the actual exercise of imperative control is so sporadic, the
possibility and propriety of its recurrence may be continually
reaffirmed in ritual. Political activity thus floats on a ritual
stream. To whom or to which role, complementary delegation
applies tends to be implicit in a segmentary lineage system, but
explicit in a segmentary state. In the former it applies to
generalized roles, for if they were politically specialized it would
necessarily be a segmentary state. In a segmentary state the
roles at the peak of the pyramid are repeated or at least adum-
brated in its subordinate components. The development of
unique political roles at the peak of the pyramid turns it into a
hierarchy and the segmentary into a unitary state.

Although recognition that the essentially segmentary aspect
of political relations is ubiquitous seems to dilute the stricter
meaning of the term segmentary, this recognition is very important and social anthropology may surely claim credit for it.
There is no need for confusion about segmentary systems, in the
stricter pyramidal sense. The segmentary lineage system, as an
ideal type, may be represented by comparatively few empirical
systems, though the Nuer and Tiv are clearly not unique
(Sahlins, 1961, p. 322).

The following meanings have to be distinguished:

I Segmentary – political (i.e. policy activity)

II A. Segmentary – pyramidal (complementary delegation)

    1. Stateless societies

       (*a*) Segmentary lineage systems

       (*b*) Age–organized societies

       (*c*) Other articulated but acephalous local com-
          munities

    2. Segmentary states

       (*a*) based on segmentary lineage systems

       (*b*) based on other forms of articulation

    3. Confederative states*

B. Segmentary – hierarchical (associational delegation)

    1. Unitary states

    2. Federal states†

* The relation between the major components is supposedly pyramidal, but their internal structure is hierarchical. Confederative states are composed of largely separate communities, whereas federal states approximate more to unitary though composite communities with special powers reserved to the components. It is thus in principle appropriate for citizenship to attach to a federal state as such but to component communities of a confederative state. Confederative states appear to be essentially unstable and short-lived in the modern world. One interesting counterpart of this is that their 'organic' structure lacks the ritual binding which a 'mechanical' structure would have.

† The relation between the major components, as well as their internal structure, is hierarchical, though it may be limited in scope.

III. THE MEANS OF GENERALIZATION

I agree with Horton (1963, p. 6) that contemporary functional analysis tends to end up with certain irreducible purposes and premises of a particular social system and that 'any further interpretation must be one that shows them as the effects of certain causes'. It is most important that the rightful insistence on the distinction between sociological and psychological frames of reference should not tacitly amount to a naïve belief that these two worlds have no common point of reference. But no amount of theoretical discussion will clarify 'those causal factors that set and change the ultimate purposes which "reason" strives to fulfil', unless structural-functional analysis, on a comparative and diachronic basis, can demonstrate such occurrences empirically.

No doubt there are periods at which major progress can be made by a kind of Copernican Revolution, when by a dialectical process of reversion new illumination can come. Doubtless the change from evolutionary to functional anthropology was such a period, though, like all revolutions, it looks more gradual and continuous the more it is studied in detail. But at the moment there is no call for Copernican Revolution, in the sense that, while our concepts certainly need greater refinement and unanimity, we have got nowhere near exploiting them to the full.

We cannot generalize because we lack the data. We lack the

data because we have not done the fieldwork. If this seems surprising, let me put it thus. Most social anthropologists have studied one or two societies intensively, to the point of ability to see them in terms of appropriate models. They have often chosen two societies not only radically different but far apart. The result is that there are hardly any instances in which the covariation of structural elements in neighbouring systems over time has been effectively studied. How much more elementary could we be? This is the crux of the structural-functional problem. We can make a model but we cannot order it. We make a refined, intensive analysis of one society which fails either because there are too many unstated assumptions or givens (as in the field of ultimate values, meanings, purposes, and goals) or because these are given interpretations which would immediately be proved false if the neighbouring society were studied.

Some detailed Amerindian studies may approach these requirements, but I suspect that in most cases the time-depth of American Indian cultures renders it impossible. Eggan's *Social Organization of the Western Pueblos* (1950) is a fine example, but he was obviously hampered as soon as he had to move outside the range in which he could control and supplement the deficient data of other investigators by his own field experience. More fundamentally, Pueblo societies appear to have diverged slowly over so long a period that historical records are not able to yield data of the refinement required by social anthropology. Leach's (1954) studies of Highland Burma would appear to be an approach. Are Goody's (1956) two societies, which Leach attributes to discrepant field notes (Leach, 1961a, p. 3), examples of another attempt? Evans-Pritchard's studies of the Zande (1937, 1963) and Nuer (1940b, 1956), which ask for this treatment in every other respect, may not be quite close enough to qualify, lacking sufficient components in common. The Nuer and Anuak (Evans-Pritchard, 1940a) provide more adequate ground, but for the fact that practical difficulties limited further study, especially in the latter case. The studies of Chilver and Kaberry on a cluster of variant groups in Cameroon also offer promising material. The recent attempt by LeVine and Sangree (1962, p. 97) to explain the adoption of age organization by the Tiriki and not by the Gusii appears to be sound as far as it goes.

But historical explanation of the borrowing of completely new institutions from one society to another is neither so interesting nor so important, though it is easier, than explanation of the more refined differences assumed by the same institution in a number of similar and perhaps genetically linked societies. The definition of age groups by LeVine and Sangree as Nilo-Hamitic is misleading, for there is no adequate evidence as yet to demonstrate whether, for example, Bantu Kikuyu borrowed from Nilo-Hamitic Masai, Masai from Kikuyu, or both from a single or several other sources (Murdock, 1959, pp. 196-203).

The point is that *differences arising from similarities* are the most fruitful field from which to derive generalizations. Study of the functional implications of minor divergence in otherwise cognate elements in several neighbouring or genetically linked social systems, or of differences in a few minor components of otherwise comparable syndromes, is now the most fundamental requirement for advancing the theory of the working of social systems. This appears to be a different emphasis from that given by Murdock (1960, pp. 183-188) in his treatment of the uses of typology, where interest is focused upon similarities and their attribution to various combinations of the processes of migration, convergence, and diffusion.

Our structural analyses will have meaning only when we can show in detail how the components of a functional system change. The logical possibilities are limited.

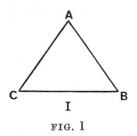

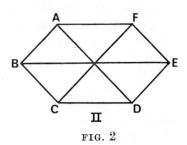

FIG. 1   FIG. 2

If the deceptively simple diagrams of *Figures 1* and *2* suggest the abstract models in which we represent the component functional elements, or factors of social structures, there are four main possibilities.

1. Factor B is a function of the other components of the system in a mathematical sense.

The system is in equilibrium and cannot change. Hence the accusation of conservative ideology in functional theory.

2. (*a*) The system is not logically closed, but only partially so. A, B, C, D, E, and F are only partially defined in terms of one another. (The partiality represents both inadequate definition and human freedom.)

(*b*) The system is logically closed, but there is a degree of play or tolerance so that each function can vary slightly without permanently upsetting the system. The equilibrium can be pushed off centre but will eventually return to it.[3] The state co-ordinates will bring it back (Cancian, 1960, p. 820). The rubber sheet can be pulled askew but will return to its original shape when tension is eased (Leach, 1961a, p. 7).

3. Unpredictable mutations occur within the system. We can at least study cases if we cannot predict them.

4. New external factors intrude. They are, of course external only in a logical, not necessarily a spatial or temporal sense. But unfortunately the 'intrusion' may in practice mean something we failed to detect rather than something essentially new.

Any intrusion which is not merely an indicator of faulty previous analysis must have a temporal aspect and therefore requires historical study. We may or may not be able to demonstrate the source of the intrusion. Epidemics, vagaries of weather, emigration, and immigration, are some of the many obvious factors. Changes of ultimate values are the common case of the intractable.

In the past we have had debate between the extreme positions of those who see social anthropology as an emergent natural science seeking laws and those who see it as a special kind of history documenting particular and unique sequences of events. The next phase in the dialectic should be not synchronic structural analysis of laws, nor unique history, but diachronic structural analysis through history to establish generalizations.

Apart from the necessary theoretical orientations, there are categorical practical implications. We still communicate with one another so badly that the objective can only be reached, if at all, by all the necessary material passing through a single intellect. This presupposes intensive fieldwork, in several languages, over several contiguous societies of common or intermingled proximate origin. This is very difficult but not impossible, especially if it is recognized as the only way of achieving certain results. It would be fatal if the edge of synchronic analysis were dulled; but also fatal if it should be thought that ethno-historians naïve in the theory of social anthropology can supply the dimension of time and change. By comparison with the potential results of such diachronic structural-functional analysis, to continue rearranging old and incomplete material in different sets of pigeon holes is indeed to fiddle while Rome burns.

Where it is impossible for the necessary fieldwork to be achieved by one person, institutional arrangements must be encouraged which will favour either long-term intimate acquaintance between those fieldworkers who collectively command the required data, or full reciprocal availability of their field notes with opportunity for detailed consultation to ensure communication. Better-defined supplementary field projects would also doubtless emerge.

Models are implicit in any effective functional analysis, models being necessarily functional on the pattern of the mathematical sense, even if their values are qualitative and relative, not quantitative or absolute, and the systems only partially closed. It is in the light of the formal properties of models that more limited and precise variables can be selected for comparison. This is not the opposite of functional analysis but a stage of it. We agree with Kingsley Davis (1959) that in this sense functional analysis is essentially the scientific method and not a special discovery of social anthropologists.

Presumably the limited number of variables which are taken out of the model, in its abstract aspect, or out of the functional nexus, in its more empirical aspect, are those which best combine and reconcile the requirements of relevance to the immediate discussion and precise definition. Such selected variables are nearly always themselves composite, therefore their artificial isolation from the other components of the system permits study of the internal factors of which they are composed. Two operations are then possible. The same composite variable will

133

be isolated from a variety of empirical systems and checked for comparability, and possible generalized propositions will be explored. It will also be put back into the systems to which it belongs, seen as far as possible in its whole context, and further recurring relationships will be noted. When the components of a model have been related to a number of empirical systems in this way, evidence will be collected as to the amount of play, or tolerance, between variables, that is, the limits of stable equilibrium. Knowledge of the behaviour of a system over a considerable period of time may be required to establish this. The more play there is, that is, apparent lack of functional dependence, the more the question arises as to whether the variables are properly defined, or whether they are not in fact independent. But in the world of social anthropology it is best to recognize how blurred the distinction between dependence and independence usually is. Absolute dependence is rarely demonstrable. Independence is a matter of degree. While independence means that the supposed variables of a system are not fully defined in terms of one another, it clearly does not mean that they are without reciprocal influence.[4] It may be agreed that, since all models are abstract; there is no reason why the model itself should not be determinate and logically closed, but I think the temptation to evade the issue would be less if the indeterminacy of the social facts was clearly represented in the model.

It is impossible to indicate adequately the variables which ought to be studied in this way to further our understanding of political systems, for this would involve a catalogue of most of the elements of social systems. But some obvious variables do cry out for study, both in their external functional aspect as composite factors and in their internal detail, such as: maximization of agnates and expansion of chiefship; the varying balance of political and ritual factors in authority; special types of succession such as positional succession; the relation between age organizations and descent systems; the relation of armed bands to types of chiefship and descent system; the ancestor cult; the consistent ecological determinants of the size, structure, isolation, and permanence of domestic groups and local communities; the history of land and resource availability in relation to conquest, expansion, and incorporation.

This discussion has been oriented mainly to Africa for obvious reasons hardly necessary to specify. Apart from a limited number of oddly distributed pockets, next to no information is readily available, in terms of our own frame of reference, for the whole of Asia and other major regions such as South America. The studies of Sahlins (1958) on Polynesia, Steward (1959) on South America, or Murdock (1960b) on Southeast Asia, are focused on different sets of problems, in other frames of reference. More elementary work at the level of typology and classification of political systems would not be out of place here, to enable others to find their way about without getting lost, in preparation for more advanced work. Such a broadening of the field would undoubtedly redress some of the biases inherent in the African material taken alone.

One of the worst biases in the African material is the tendency to a simple dichotomy between supposedly primeval systems, stated in the ethnographic present, and the contemporary situation. The latter is left to be studied only at the centre, by political scientists with inadequate knowledge of language or understanding of the general social context. Schapera (1956, p. 8) actually states 'by a "political community" I mean a group of people organized into a single unit managing its affairs independently of control (except that exercised nowadays by European governments)'. What sort of a universal definition is it that depends upon such an exception? A breath of reality must be introduced by recognition that African peoples have often passed through a number of significant phases: the traditional, Arab, German, British, and Independent periods of the Nyamwezi in Tanganyika (Abrahams, 1962); the traditional, Turkish, British, and Independent Sudanese periods of the Shilluk; or the aboriginal, Slave-caravan and Portuguese and Civil War periods of the Ovimbundu. In a study of local political structure in India, there would presumably be less temptation to view it otherwise than in its contemporary and historical dimensions in an empirical fashion.

Many of us have been involved in the paradoxical irony that some of the most interesting and theoretically stimulating African political systems have been studied, as it were in amber, when they had almost ceased to exist. The real context of

135

African political life has often been uninteresting to us, because it was colonial, as we were, therefore supposedly familiar.

This temptation is passing and it is to be hoped that a reorientation of interest will be noticeable. Independent African states will increase pressure at some points on local community structure and reduce it at many others. The overall structure itself, though obviously adapted from Western models, will become less and less familiar, less to be taken for granted, and more worthy of study in its interaction with ethnically diverse, formerly tribal, local groups. The theoretical problems of analysis will be more complicated, but cannot be evaded any longer by ventures into unreality.

Any unidimensional typology is relevant only to a partial analysis, vital to the understanding of particular sets of factors, but inappropriate to others which also require interpretation. As soon as a particular typology acquires an exclusive aura it becomes an obstacle to further analysis and understanding.

At the risk of redundancy, I would like to set out in crude detail, for readers in other disciplines, one possible statement of the successive practical steps involved in structural-functional analysis on a comparative and diachronic basis by the social anthropologist. It is easy to agree with Kingsley Davis that functional analysis is simply scientific method, but it is the practical steps involved which are most rarely achieved.

Comparative, diachronic, structural-functional analysis

1. Intimate, intensive, fieldwork knowledge of two or more societies and the models of their organizational ideas.

2. The several societies should be cognate, to permit the study of concomitant variation.

3. That is, the initial model is put through a series of transformations, corresponding to the several societies.

4. If the several transformations properly represent the abstract qualities of the several societies, then, by changing the pattern of component factors, or altering their relative strength, or substituting one for another while the rest are held constant,

the transformations demonstrate the degree of dependence of one factor on another, that is, its function.

5. The several *spatial* transformations, which correspond to the several cognate societies, must be matched by *temporal* transformations corresponding to the changes which have occurred or may occur in the several societies.

6. Changes can thus be traced to their antecedent causes, without or within the system in which they have occurred.

7. This will provide only proximate, not ultimate explanation, but is the next advance possible to the anthropologist.

8. If the spatial and temporal transformations are correctly ordered they provide reciprocally corroborative evidence.

9. The study of such spatial and temporal transformations offers the only valid possibility of injecting some comprehension of meaning and purpose into functional analysis.

10. The transformations also indicate where change has occurred for non-sociological reasons and can identify the points of contact of sociological and psychological frames of reference without confusion.

11. A final argument for this approach is that if we become practised at it we shall be able to cope more adequately with social systems which we cannot pretend to be static.[5]

NOTES

1. For example, Logoli, Tallensi, Kiga, Gisu, Iraqw, Lugbara, Turkana, and large areas of what is now Southern Tanganyika.

2. Organic is the convenient shorthand for a familiar idea, although the concept of a continuum of role differentiation is theoretically preferable.

3. Examples of this are Bohannan's 'anti-tsav' movements among the Tiv which he suggests recurred cyclically without permanently altering the structure of the society (Bohannan, 1958).

4. E.g. 'Different forms of avunculate can co-exist with one and the same type of descent, patrilineal or matrilineal' (R. Needham, 1962, quoting Lévi-Strauss, 1958, pp. 50, 51, 52, 55).

5. A useful exercise at this stage would be to examine some of the promising bodies of material to see how far these steps have been or can be carried out. This was attempted in the original version of the paper, but cannot be contained within the necessary compass.

REFERENCES

Names of journals are abbreviated as follows:

AA   *American Anthropologist*
ASR   *American Sociological Review*
JRAI *Journal of the Royal Anthropological Institute*

ABRAHAMS, R. G. 1962. Unpublished Ph.D. thesis, Cambridge.
BOHANNAN, P. 1958. Extra-Processual Events in Tiv Political Institutions. *AA* **60**: 1-12.
CANCIAN, F. 1960. Functional Analysis of Change. *ASR* **25**: 818-827.
DAVIS, K. 1959. The Myth of Functional Analysis. *ASR* **24**: 757-772.
EASTON, D. 1953. *The Political System*. New York: Knopf.
EGGAN, F. 1950. *Social Organization of the Western Pueblos*. Chicago: University of Chicago Press.
EVANS-PRITCHARD, E. E. 1937. *Witchcraft, Oracles and Magic among the Azande*. Oxford: Clarendon Press.
—— 1940a. *The Political System of the Anuak of the Anglo-Egyptian Sudan*. LSE Monographs, London: Athlone Press.
—— 1940b. The Nuer of the Southern Sudan. In Fortes, M. & Evans-Pritchard, E. E. (1940).
—— 1956. *Nuer Religion*. Oxford: Clarendon Press.
—— 1963. The Zande State. *JRAI* **93**: 134-154.
FORTES, M. & EVANS-PRITCHARD, E. E. 1940. *African Political Systems*. London: Oxford University Press.
FREEMAN, J. D. 1958. The Family System of the Iban of Borneo. In Goody, J. (ed.), (1958).
FRIED, M. H. 1957. The Classification of Corporate Unilineal Descent Groups. *JRAI* **87**: 1-30.
GLUCKMAN, M. (ed.). 1962. *Essays on the Ritual of Social Relations*. Manchester: Manchester University Press.
GOODY, J. 1956. *The Social Organization of the Lowiili*. London: HMSO.
—— (ed.) 1958. *The Developmental Cycle in Domestic Groups*. Cambridge: Cambridge University Press.
GULLIVER, P. H. 1963. *Social Control in an African Society*. London: Routledge & Kegan Paul.
HORTON, W. R. G. 1963. The Boundaries of Explanation in Social Anthropology. *Man* **63**, No. 6.

Typology of States and Political Systems

KABERRY, P. M. 1959. Traditional Government in Nsaw. *Africa* 29: 366-383.

—— 1962. Retainers and Royal Households in the Cameroons Grassfields. *Cahiers d'études africaines* 3: 282-298.

KARBERRY, P. M. & CHILVER, E. M. 1960. From Tribute to Tax in a Tikar Chiefdom. *Africa* 30: 1-18.

—— 1961. An Outline of the Traditional Political System of Bali-Nyonga. *Africa* 31: 355-371.

—— 1963. Traditional Government in Bafut, West Cameroon. *Nigerian Field* 28: 4-30.

KLUCKHOHN, C. 1960. The use of Typology in Anthropological Theory. In Wallace, A. F. C. (1960).

LEACH, E. R. 1954. *Political Systems of Highland Burma*. London: Bell.

—— 1961a. *Rethinking Anthropology*. London: Athlone Press.

—— 1961b. *Pul Eliya*. Cambridge: Cambridge University Press.

LIENHARDT, R. G. 1961. *Divinity and Experience*. Oxford: Clarendon Press.

LEVINE R. & SANGREE, W. 1962. The Diffusion of Age-Group Organization in East Africa: A Controlled Comparison. *Africa* 32: 97.

LÉVI-STRAUSS, C. 1953. Social Structure. In A. L. Kroeber (ed.), *Anthropology Today*. Chicago: University of Chicago Press.

—— 1958. *Anthropologie Structurale*. Paris.

MAIR, L. P. 1962. *Primitive Government*. Harmondsworth: Penguin Books.

MERTON, R. K. 1957. *Social Theory and Social Structure*. Glencoe, Ill.: The Free Press.

MIDDLETON, J. 1960. *Lugbara Religion*. London: Oxford University Press.

MURDOCK, G. P. 1949. *Social Structure*. New York: Macmillan.

—— 1959. *Africa, Its Peoples and their Culture History*. New York: McGraw-Hill.

—— 1960a. Typology in the Area of Social Organization. In Wallace, A. F. C. (1960).

—— (ed.). 1960b. *Social Structure in Southeast Asia*. Viking Fund Publications in Anthropology No. 29. Chicago: Quadrangle Books; London: Tavistock Publications.

NEEDHAM, R. 1962. *Structure and Sentiment*. Chicago: University of Chicago Press.

PARK. G. K. 1962. The Problem of late marriage of Kinga women. East African Institute of Social Research Conference Paper.

RADCLIFFE-BROWN, A. R. 1940. In Fortes, M. & Evans-Pritchard, E. E. (eds.), *African Political Systems* (1940).

RADCLIFFE-BROWN, A. R. & FORDE, C.D. (eds.). 1950. *African Systems of Kinship and Marriage.* London: Oxford University Press.

RICHARDS, A. I. 1950. Some Types of Family Structure among the Central Bantu. In Radcliffe-Brown, A. R. & Forde, C. D. (1950).

SAHLINS, M. (1958). *Social Stratification in Polynesia.* Seattle: University of Washington Press.

—— 1961. The Segmentary Lineage: An Organization of Predatory Expansion. *AA* **63**: 322.

SCHAPERA, I. 1956. *Government and Politics in Tribal Societies.* London: Watts.

SMITH, M. G. 1956. On Segmentary Lineage Systems. *JRAI*: **86**, 39-80.

SOUTHALL, A. W. 1956. *Alur Society.* Cambridge: Heffer.

—— 1959. An Operational Theory of Role. *Human Relations* **12**: 17-34.

STEWARD, J. H. & FARON, L. C. 1959. *Native Peoples of South America.* New York: McGraw-Hill.

VANSINA, J. L. 1962. A Comparison of African Kingdoms. *Africa* **32**: 324-335.

WALLACE, A. F. C. (ed.). 1960. *Selected Papers* of the Fifth International Congress of Anthropological and Ethnological Sciences, Philadelphia.

WEBER, M. 1947. *The Theory of Social and Economic Organization.* Trans. A. R. Henderson and Talcott Parsons. London: Hodge.

NOTES ON CONTRIBUTORS

BAILEY, FREDERICK GEORGE. Born 1924, England; educated at Oxford University, B.A., B.Litt.; Manchester, Ph.D.

Assistant in Social Anthropology, Manchester University, 1950; Treasury Studentship 1951–55; Lecturer in Asian Anthropology, School of Oriental and African Studies, London University, 1956-61; Reader in Asian Anthropology, London University, 1961-64; Visiting Professor, Rochester University, 1963, and Chicago University, 1964; Professor of Anthropology, University of Sussex, 1964.

Author of *Caste and the Economic Frontier*, 1957; *Tribe, Caste and Nation*, 1960; *Politics and Social Change: Orissa in 1959*, 1964.

EGGAN, FRED. Born 1906, Seattle, Washington; studied at The University of Chicago, B.A., M.A., Ph.D.

Harold H. Swift, Distinguished Service Professor of Anthropology and Director, Philippine Studies Program, University of Chicago.

Author of *Social Organization of the Western Pueblos*. 1950; 'Social Anthropology and the Method of Controlled Comparison' (*American Anthropologist*, Vol. 56, 1954); 'Social Anthropology: Methods and Results' (in *Social Anthropology of North American Tribes*, 1955);

Editor of *Social Anthropology of North American Tribes*, 1937, Enlarged Edition, 1955.

GLUCKMAN, MAX. Born 1911, South Africa; studied at The University of Witwatersrand, B.A.; Oxford, D.Phil.

Anthropologist, Rhodes-Livingstone Institute, 1939-42; Director, 1942-47; Lecturer in Social Anthropology, Oxford, 1947-49; Professor of Social Anthropology, Manchester, 1949.

Author of *The Judicial Process among the Barotse of N. Rhodesia*, 1954; *Custom and Conflict in Africa*, 1955; *Order and Rebellion in Tribal Africa*, 1963; *Rule, Law and Ritual in Tribal Societies*, 1964; *The Ideas of Barotse Jurisprudence*, 1964. Editor of *Seven Tribes of British Central Africa*, 1951; *Closed Systems and Open Minds*, 1964.

LLOYD, PETER C. Born 1927, United Kingdom; studied at Oxford University, B.A. (Geography), B.Sc., D.Phil. (Social Anthropology).

Research Fellow, West African Institute of Social and

Economic Research, Ibadan, 1950; Land Research Officer, Western Nigeria Government, 1956; Lecturer in Sociology, University College, Ibadan, 1959; Senior Lecturer, 1962; Senior Lecturer in Sociology (West Africa), University of Birmingham, 1964.

Author of *Yoruba Land Law,* 1962.

NICHOLAS, RALPH WALLACE. Born 1934, U.S.A.; educated at Wayne State University, B.A.; University of Chicago, M.A., Ph.D.

Ford Foundation Foreign Area Training Fellow, 1960-61; Research Fellow, School of Oriental and African Studies, London University, 1962; Assistant Professor, Portland State College, 1963; Assistant Professor, Michigan State University, 1964.

SOUTHALL, AIDAN WILLIAM. Born 1920, England; educated at Cambridge University, B.A.; London, Ph.D.

Lecturer in Social Studies, Makerere College, Uganda, 1945-48; Colonial Research Fellow, 1949-51; Senior Research appointments in East African Institute of Social Research, 1951-57; Professor of Sociology and Social Anthropology, Makerere College and Chairman of E.A.I.S.R., 1957; Dean of the Faculty of Social Sciences, 1963-64; Professor of Anthropology, Syracuse University, New York, 1964.

Author of *Alur Society,* 1956; joint author of *Townsmen in the Making,* 1957; editor, *Social Change in Modern Africa,* 1961.